Dating Vegans
Recipes for Relationships

Anne Dinshah

First Edition: March 2012
ISBN: 978-0-942401-20-2

Published by:
American Vegan Society
56 Dinshah Lane, PO Box 369
Malaga, NJ 08328 U.S.A.

Printed in the United States of America on recycled paper.

Cover design by Carolyn Githens. Cover and inside photos of Oliver and Anne by Jessica Lutkenhouse. Inside photos of Dude and Barb, Paul, Hank, Philip, Jeff, and Steve by the author. Jay and Freya by Victory Studio. Nick and Adair by Jonathan Valentin. William and Victoria by Monica McCarthy. Daniel and Heidi by Jennie Kerwood. Maribeth and other couples' photos supplied by the subjects. Author's photo by Linda Long.

to Paul Bergman

Acknowledgments

I value people more than stories, and I am fortunate to have encountered many wonderful people along this flavorful journey. Thank you to all the men who contributed to this project. I appreciate the inspirations, food, fun, memories, and ongoing friendships I have shared with Todd Alexander, Steve Becker, Paul Bergman, Jim Bidigare, Robert Crane, Gabriel Figueroa, Guy George, Hank Hawkins, Brad Holdren, Tony Kozlowski, Loren Lockman, Michael Main, Dave Nagel, Jeff Parimuha, Philip Spinks, Chris Weisbeck, Mike Wojtkowiak, and many other friends.

Thank you to all the couples who shared their stories: Ed Coffin and George Sampson, Randall and Debbie Collura, Heidi and Daniel Fox, Dude Hamre and Barb Johnson, Kim Johnson and Rusty Gardner, Jennie and Dan Kerwood, Adair and Nick Moran, Victoria Moran and William Melton, Jo and Michael Stepaniak, and Anne and Angus Watkins.

Special thanks to the couple who set me on a great path in life—my parents, Freya and H. Jay Dinshah. They showed me what it is like to truly share your life with someone, how to prepare and enjoy great vegan meals, and how to work to improve the world together.

Thank you to Lee Martin and the English 568, spring 2009 class at The Ohio State University for inviting me to join discussions of creative nonfiction writing.

Thank you to Maribeth Abrams, Wenona Dege, Carolyn Githens, Sue Holmes, Cynthia Holzapfel, Ellen Koenig, Linda Long, Jennifer Loshark, Jessica Lutkenhouse, and Cheryl Redmond for your suggestions, perspectives on relationships, encouragement, brainstorming, and friendship.

Thank you to everyone who has tested my recipes and provided feedback. Let's dine together again soon. You may cook.

And finally, my biggest thank you to Oliver Claypool for having the courage and fortitude to be a date, a friend, a muse, and an Oliver.

Contents

Introduction

Dating: Dating encompasses any preplanned social interaction between two people. It is usually, but not necessarily, romantic in nature.

Vegans: Vegans (pronounced VEE-guns) are people who avoid animal products for ethical, health, and environmental reasons. Their diet, derived from a variety of vegetables, grains, legumes, fruits, nuts, and seeds is a taste adventure, while their compassionate choices also extend to clothing and other products.

Recipes for Relationships: You don't have to be a vegan to date a vegan.

I gave my friend Paul a copy of my vegan cookbook *Healthy Hearty Helpings*. As he flipped through the pages he asked, "Where are the meat dishes?"

"There aren't any."

"Hmmm. What's your next book?"

"Well, I'm thinking about *Cooking Vegan for My Meat-Eating Friends*."

"Why not *Cooking Meat for My Meat-Eating Friends*?" he jested, poker-faced.

"I'm vegan. I don't know how to cook meat! When are you coming to dinner? Tonight?"

"No thanks. I'm having a PowerBar."

Paul is a rugged, healthy, confident guy who appears afraid of nothing. But perhaps he feared the unknown . . . a vegan meal.

Lots of people have never eaten a meal with a vegan, although they have eaten vegan meals any time there were only plant products on their plate. What if they had to confront their apprehension to enjoy a meal with a vegan friend? What if they actually dated a vegan or had a long-term relationship with one and had to conquer their fear? What if they had never before thought about their food choices and now have begun to ask questions? And what if a vegan were to fall in love with a meat eater—would the relationship be doomed from the start, or could love and compassion triumph?

Dating Vegans is a unique nonfiction collection of personal stories from real people. My stories as a lifetime vegan who chooses to date nonvegan men exposed a myriad of issues while I searched for a great relationship. Food choices and discussions enhanced my dating instead of hindering the time together. Questions arose for both vegans and nonvegans to ponder and solve if the dates were to get serious. Fortunately my friends who are in successful long-term relationships of "mixed" couples (typically one person is vegan while the other is or was nonvegan) provide inspirations for people with different philosophies to find happiness together.

This book is for both vegans and nonvegans who are interested in dating each other, or for those already in a relationship with someone who maintains contradictory consumptions. Nonvegans will gain insights into the beliefs and concerns of vegans. Vegans will find ideas and strategies for patiently sharing their values. The nonvegans in this book vouch for the delicious vegan recipes which will entice both parties to enter the kitchen.

May all those who open this book embark on great culinary and romantic adventures!

Philosophy on Dating and Vegans

The Ingredients

Friendship Versus Dating

Humans are social by nature. Both friendship and dating provide companionship, but the word "dating" is off-putting to some people because it can imply commitment, exclusivity, romance, or sexual involvement.

Relationships have a variety of forms, from casual acquaintances to best buddies. Regardless of the type of relationship, those that endure have something in common: unconditional love. This type of deep caring—the kind that is totally accepting, warts and all—can be shared between two people whether they are "just friends" or "more than friends." The people I love may not always make the same choices that I do, but we acknowledge and respect each other's decisions anyway. Perhaps that is why most of the men I have dated in the past still consider me their friend. We can offer each other our opinions, but even when we disagree, our relationship survives because of our abiding, mutual respect.

Some people I know think that hanging out with my friends is a waste of my time that could be better spent looking for romance. I don't believe that having friends precludes me from having a romantic relationship; love and friendship are not mutually exclusive. I am confident that I can have both and that each one of my relationships enriches my life. I often meet wonderful people through my friends or their friends, or by engaging in activities I would not normally do by myself.

When I started writing this book, I joked with friends that it was ironic for me to be writing about dating, since I'm not really very good at it. I just like developing recipes for a new date. My views have evolved since then, and I now realize that I am actually very successful at dating. I quickly know when I have connected with someone as a friend or a date, and whether my attraction is physical, emotional, intellectual, or a combination of all of these. The basic ingredients for being a great friend are the same ones required to be a great date: honesty, enthusiasm, patience, communication (especially being a good listener), participation, sense of humor, tolerance, optimism, and reliability. Honing these skills with friends will increase your odds of being an excellent date when the opportunity arises.

I have unusually high standards for myself and for those who are my closest friends or who want to date me. My mom once told me, "It is not about finding the man you can live with; it's about finding the one you can't live without." Most of my friends are single men. Perhaps that's because I like sports and construction work and detest shopping. Or maybe it's because I try to share my thoughts tactfully but honestly. Then again, maybe it's because I'm attracted to the wonderful qualities each one of my friends possesses. Perhaps the best way to meet a terrific guy is to know one . . . or many. Great romances frequently develop when we are not looking for them.

Oliver (p. 81) and Anne share grapes in the park.

I am Vegan

Somewhere early in conversations with people I first meet they often say, "You look great! What do you do?"

I typically reply, "I have a great job. I coach rowing. I get paid to work out." If I leave it at that, we will talk about employment or exercise. Depending on my mood, I sometimes also say, "I'm vegetarian." This always prompts a comment about food choices, including the five most common responses:

"Are you a vegan?"

"I eat less red meat than I used to."

"I should eat better. You could help me."

"That's cool."

"I like meat."

I have encountered each of these replies so often that my thoughts and reactions are almost automatic, especially when the comment comes from a man:

"Are you a vegan?" I can judge from the tone of his voice whether he thinks my being vegan is great or whether he is looking for a debate, which is something I do not engage in with people I just met. If he seems to be looking for an argument, I simply say, "I choose to be vegan." Most people will respect that. If he seems interested or impressed, then I say, "Yes, I'm vegan. Thank you for asking." He will then usually open up and talk about someone else he knows who is vegan, or perhaps even mention a time when he tried being vegan himself. Maybe he is looking for a way to be cool like me. If so, we are off to a good start.

"I eat less red meat than I used to." If a cute guy told me this, I might think he has potential. He probably has never tried being vegan, and it's possible he could be a future vegan. Plus he will typically respect my choice.

"I should eat better. You could help me." This is actually one of the worst responses I hear because it reveals that the man has some knowledge but poor willpower. I want to date someone who respects himself and makes intelligent decisions. If he seems terrific in other ways, though, maybe he stands half a chance.

"That's cool." This is a respectable response that usually segues into other topics for conversation. The subject of food will arise again when we get hungry.

"I like meat." If the guy is someone I am not too interested in, or if I notice from his tone of voice or body language that he is looking for a debate, I might respond by saying, "We each make our own choices." However, if he relays this comment with a warm, mischievous smile and I am intrigued by his other characteristics, I might be interested in taking things further. He has not experienced my cooking yet, so I might ask, "What are your three favorite vegetables?" This often leads to some engaging dialogue.

My friendships and dates are typically with nonvegans. I am completely vegan when I am at home and as close to that as possible when I go out. I do not compromise my core values, but a tiny bit of flexibility allows me to build bridges with nonvegans, instead of walls. It also prevents me from getting stressed out. Because I was raised as a vegan, I have no fond memories of animal products and no cravings for them. If someone says an item tastes phenomenal I may have a taste and then develop a vegan version. "Doing research" is a conscious ethical decision I make.

I enjoy eating out with my nonvegan friends at their homes or at restaurants, and in return they like to experience vegan meals I make. The vegan bounty has never failed to shatter the myth that vegans eat only grass and twigs, and many of my friends have been inspired to try their hand in the kitchen with me.

Dating in our society often involves sharing meals. Vegan recipes can be simple, delicious, fun, and even romantic to make and eat. Discussing veganism and preparing vegan food together can quickly move two people beyond superficial dating fluff to a deeper and more dynamic connection.

Desirable Qualities in a Partner

The desirable qualities of people we like to date are those characteristics that make them appealing to us. For a growing number of people, being vegan tops that list. Everyone has the potential to be a vegan; most people just do not know that yet.

I knew I would date many meat-eating men in my research for this book. Although I have dated vegans and nonvegans in the past, I chose to only have interest in nonvegans for this year. I wondered if it would bother me to focus on exploring divergent food interests. I hoped it would not prohibit me from finding someone wonderful. Perhaps it would lead to the right man for me.

Curious to know if "vegan" is in my top ten list of requirements, I brainstormed a list of the qualities I look for in a man I would like to date (I did not include the obvious: single, common interests, approachable, and physical attraction) and then filed it away. I did not look at the list again until I finished writing the manuscript.

Reviewing the list now, I can think of a few additional qualities, such as "good communicator," which are essential to a relationship. Nevertheless, here is the original list of the characteristics I most prefer in a datable man:

1. intelligent
2. athletic
3. healthy
4. makes good decisions
5. honest and trustworthy
6. responsible & accountable
7. hard-working, with a sense of purpose
8. energetic
9. fond of children
10. witty and humorous
11. compassionate
12. organized
13. fun
14. confident
15. good-tempered
16. vegan

Although "vegan" is the sixteenth quality, it doesn't mean that I want to date someone who is openly antagonistic toward vegans. Although I grew up having the benefit of being vegan, I'm aware that most Americans were raised to eat whatever food their parents served them. Now, as an adult, I am comfortable and confident that being vegan is the right choice for me, the animals, and the planet. Most people have not been exposed to the information about veganism that has been such an integral part of my background. Many people can make strides toward better health, compassionate cooking, and helping the environment. It is important for me to set a positive, friendly example.

If a man is intelligent, athletic, and healthy, it makes reasonable sense that he would like to learn more about his food choices. If eating meals with me exposes him to new options, I have planted vegan seeds, even if our relationship fizzles.

A man who is intelligent has the ability to be an independent thinker and is usually open to learning. Athletic men are not only fit but are also customarily interested in their overall health, particularly exercise and food choices. Intelligence combined with an interest in health lends itself to curiosity about veganism. A man who makes good decisions makes the best choices possible based on the information available to him at the time. True change happens when someone wants to change. I can only help facilitate a path towards veganism by providing information. We can walk the path together during dates.

I asked my vegan male friends what they look for in a woman. Many prefer to date only vegans, but understand the reality that in certain areas of the country that means they would be alone. Many of the qualities that lend themselves to an interest in veganism are high on their lists. Besides the obvious physical attraction, chemistry, and some common interests, most look for women who are **intelligent, athletic,** and **healthy**, which parallels my top three. Their lists commonly include **compassionate, spiritual, good-humored,** and **witty**. **Vegan** averages around the fifth quality when not the first quality.

Brainstorming with female vegan friends revealed they look for similar qualities to what vegan men seek; gender does not seem to determine different qualities a vegan looks for in a partner.

Philosophy

Nonvegans typically do not list vegan or nonvegan on their lists of desirable qualities in a partner. If a vegan has lots of terrific qualities, nonvegans are often open to trying some vegan food and discussing solutions. Vegans should not be expected to partake in nonvegan food because they have already made a commitment to their strong beliefs. Compatible options abound when a couple wants to be together. For ideas on how to negotiate a long-term relationship between a vegan and a nonvegan, read about couples who make it work on pages 144, 147, 158, and 164.

Anne feeds Jeff (p. 73) his new favorite pie, Pumpkin Medley.

Dating Vegans

Tips for Dating a Vegan

Partners in a vegan/nonvegan relationship are more differentiated by their food choices than gender. Therefore the information presented in this book can be helpful to either sex. However, in acknowledgement of some gender differences, the following separate lists are provided although many ideas will work in a relationship with any vegan. The "chicks" list was compiled from conversations with numerous vegan women as well as a few nonvegans who have dated them. Vegan men divulged what has worked, works, or will work for them on the "hunks" list.

Top Ten Tips for Dating a Vegan Chick

1. Respect her values and beliefs, even though you may not agree with or understand them yet.
2. Find an organic farmer's market and suggest going there together. A farmer's market is a good place to take a stroll and be inspired by the vegetables.
3. Suggest a food-shopping date. Learn which common foods are objectionable and how to find alternatives. Make a game of finding out how many seconds it takes you to spot the nonvegan item in an ingredient list or the acceptable vegan product. (This can be combined with the next tip.)
4. Make dinner together. Find a vegan recipe from this book that you would like to try.
5. Show your soft side occasionally (even tough men have one). Suggest a day trip to an animal sanctuary or volunteer together at an animal shelter.
6. Give her gifts, especially ones that represent your feelings and values, or your understanding of hers. For example, if you want to give her chocolates, check the ingredients because even dark chocolate may contain dairy products. You could wrap the box in a scarf of her favorite color instead of using wrapping paper; that shows your creativity and concern for the environment. Make sure the scarf is not made of animal products (such as silk or wool). Some people

believe the greatest gift is time shared together; others prefer to additionally receive a few tangible items.

7. Make homemade vegan cookies or another vegan treat. A special treat made with loving care will always be delicious.

8. Inquire about her lifestyle because you are genuinely interested. When you are ready, suggest watching slaughterhouse footage or an animal rights documentary, and be prepared to challenge your assumptions. The film you watch may seem like the best horror film you have ever seen, but this is real! Careful; it may be a mood-killer for the evening. (If you truly enjoyed the "horror film," a vegan is not the right person for you to date.)

9. Research vegan, vegetarian, or vegetarian-friendly restaurants in your area (ethnic restaurants are often a good bet) and invite her out to dinner. You might ask her to select two vegan dinners that you can both share.

10. Take a gift of vegan treats or toys for her animal companions. Spend quality time playing with them.

Remember that vegan women, like all women, appreciate attention, courtesy, respect, kindness, a sense of humor, and feeling special. So do all the usual things you would do on a "normal" date. Be yourself. And occasionally try something spontaneous and different just for fun. Even something as corny as lip-synching a romantic song such as Josh Turner's "Would You Go With Me" could create a lasting impression on her.

Top Three Tips to Score with a Vegan Chick

1. Give her a fabulous massage.

2. Learn about veganism and show sincere interest in vegan issues. Ask questions without being antagonistic. If you turn her on intellectually, you have a good chance of turning her on in other ways.

3. Take a pint of nondairy ice cream when you go to pick her up. She will put it in her freezer, and you can check on its status at the end of the date.

Top Nine Ways to Get Dumped by a Vegan Chick

(These may also send many vegan hunks running in the opposite direction.)
1. Eat animal products in her presence and say, "Yum, blood!"
2. Kiss her after eating meat, without brushing your teeth.
3. Wear your full-leather outfit and give her a skimpy matching outfit, trimmed in fur.
4. Intentionally slip something not vegan into her food.
5. Offer her food with unknown ingredients.
6. Take her to a circus with lots of animal acts.
7. Give her jewelry containing pearls, bone, or leather.
8. Ask her to help you mount your trophy deer head.
9. Have silk sheets on your bed that coordinate with your wool blanket, down comforter, and feather pillows.

Twelve Steps to Win a Vegan Hunk

1. Take an interest in his beliefs and how he eats. Ask questions. Incorporate more vegan foods into your diet.
2. Take him out for a vegan meal.
3. Meet him for a smoothie. Then go on a shopping tour to a health food store, farmer's market, or supermarket. Ask lots of questions; read ingredient labels together. The print is really small, which gives you the perfect opportunity to get close. Buy the ingredients for a future dinner and dessert.
4. Cook with him. Share the tasting spoon.
5. Deliver him some homemade vegan treats. Invite him out for a surprise.
6. Take him for a ride in the country. Hike into the wilderness, impressing him with your knowledge and appreciation of nature. "Did you hear that pileated woodpecker?" When you reach the top of a scenic overlook or the bottom of a secluded waterfall, spread out a hemp blanket and serve a vegan picnic from your backpack.
7. Embrace the child within: bounce on a trampoline, go to a playground, build a snowman or sandcastle, go sledding. Laugh together.

8. Finger feed each other with ripe, succulent fruit. When appropriate, serve the fruit with your teeth, sharing every last drop from your mouths.

9. Plan an evening of strip poker, strip chess, or Twister followed by a candle-lit hot tub.

10. Lip-synch his favorite mood-setting song such as Grace Potter and the Nocturnals' "If I Was From Paris."

11. Send a text or email to build his anticipation for your next rendezvous. Feel free to use riddles and sexual innuendo liberally.

12. Go vegan! Be genuinely sure that this is something you are into, not just for him. If you have no interest in venturing towards veganism, discuss your feelings and perhaps you should just be friends. Vegan men often want to be with someone compassionate who wants to maximize her health, wellness, and overall functioning in every way.

How to Create Vegan Meals
Loved by Meat-Eating Dates

Key Questions

It's helpful to have a few key questions prepared in advance to help break the ice, especially on a first date. Here are my favorites:

Which three words would your friends use to describe you?
If you couldn't work at your current job, what kind of work would you do instead?
Where in the world would you most want to live and why?
What are your three favorite vegetables?

Casually slip in that last one to avoid immediate suspicion of a food roadblock. Rather than put a meat-eating date on the defensive or start debating incorrect notions about veganism, I prefer to dazzle him with delicious vegan food. Both people get hungry, and the question about vegetables can provide valuable insight into the potential for a relationship. Here's how this question played out with three of my dates.

Gary

"What are your three favorite vegetables?"

"Seriously, three vegetables? Can I have an easier question?"

"Can you even name three vegetables?" I was joking with him, but he quickly changed the subject.

The next time I approached the topic of vegetables, we decided we should go to the grocery store and wander the produce aisle together. I figured that I could pick out a vegetable and tell him the name of it; he could tell me whether he would consider eating it. We discontinued getting to know each other better before ever making the trip to the store. Sometimes it's smart to realize when too much opposite is not so attractive. Gary remains a friend who has never had a dinner date with me.

Jeff

Jeff answered my three-veggie question with, "Only three favorite vegetables? I like so many!"

"Well then, tell me a few."

"No, you asked specifically for three. I'm going with the green ones, the yellow ones, and the orange ones."

"Great answer!" However, I like more of a challenge, so we eased into a maybe-see-you-around friendship before I could make him an every-veggie-available stew. A few months later, Jeff contacted me and didn't remember his previous answer to the veggie question. He sparked my interest with his new response, "Broccoli, carrots, and cauliflower." (See Jeff's story, page 73.)

Ike

Ike replied to my veggie question, "Broccoli, peas, and spinach."

I met Ike at a sporting event. We spoke on the phone a few times over the next two weeks and flirted with text messages. We decided that the following Saturday would be good for dinner and dancing with friends. I wanted more information to create our dinner.

"What's your favorite fruit?" I inquired.

"All are good. Mmm . . . peaches. I love fruit! Hey, you're not a v-v-vegetarian are you?"

"Yes."

"Uh, you don't have to make dinner for me," he said, with a strange tone to his voice. Up until that moment, he had always sounded happy to talk with me.

"I want to. I like to cook. I'll make dishes we both will enjoy. What type of dessert do you like?" I asked, hoping to alleviate his concern.

"Cheesecake. Or strawberry shortcake."

"Great! I have some excellent ideas for dinner."

"I'm looking forward to seeing you Saturday!" he confirmed.

The next day I received a text message from Ike. He had forgotten his relative's graduation party on Saturday. He apologized and asked to reschedule. I left him two messages suggesting other possibilities. I never heard back from him.

Meals that are vegetarian, let alone vegan, may be intimidating to most meat eaters. Although Ike tried to convey his interest in dinner, his tone when he spoke the word "vegetarian" revealed his fear. I reevaluated my pre-dinner-date quiz and revised it to include the following three questions:

What are your three favorite vegetables?

What types of desserts do you like?

Is there any food you dislike or have an allergy to?

The question about the three vegetables gives ideas for the main focus of dinner. If the person rattles off an extensive list of vegetables, add, "Wow! Is there any vegetable you have never eaten but would like to try?" My dates Dave and Philip love most vegetables but had never eaten eggplant and beets, respectively (p. 59, 54). Now they have.

Most people love dessert and appreciate having the option to veto specific ingredients. Once you have the main dish and dessert sorted out, you will only need one other item to complete the meal: a salad, a soup, or a side dish.

Although the customary recommendation is to prepare for others dishes that you have some experience making, I tend to ignore this advice. Sometimes I end up more anxious about the meal I am going to serve than I am about my appearance. I am just as likely to forget that sprig of parsley as I am the necklace. Ah, the rapture of a good presentation!

Learning to Cook

Learning to cook takes time, but it is well worth the effort. We eat every day, so there are lots of opportunities to experiment with food preparation.

It can be helpful if you learn to cook from a friend who makes simple vegan recipes or by attending a vegan cooking class. Buy a book of easy recipes and try several of them or perfect one or two specialties.

Begin by making one main dish for a date. You can always purchase a prepared appetizer, such as pita bread and hummus, and a dessert, such as nondairy ice cream with fruit. Half of the recipes in this book are main dishes. Let dates Hank or Brad suggest one for you! (p. 47, 65)

Although cooking for yourself can be enjoyable and rewarding, it doesn't compare to the satisfaction and pride you may experience when you cook for someone else. If the other person appreciates your food and efforts, do it again. If your date is too critical, invite the person to do the cooking next time or look for someone else to date.

Tips for Novice Cooks

Recipe books are typically written for people with experience in the kitchen. Here are some basic things I would find helpful if I were a novice cook attempting Dating Vegans recipes.

Ingredient Preparation:

Wash and trim all fresh vegetables and fruits. You never know exactly where it has been—what animal has peed on it or unsanitary hands have touched it, and you want to wash off dirt and any pesticide residues. It may be necessary to trim off outside leaves, or tops or ends of vegetables. Also trim off any suspicious bad spots. Recipes don't usually tell you washing or trimming instructions. Below are my standard washing and trimming recommendations.

Blackberries and raspberries—If picked by hand at a known location, you might choose not to wash the berries. If you do decide to wash them, swish them gently in a bowl of cold water just before eating. Be extremely careful or they will fall apart.

Blueberries—Blueberries often come in a perforated container, so they may be washed by running water over them in that container. Otherwise, swish berries in a bowl of water, then pour into a colander or strainer to drain. Remove stems and any spoiled or squished berries.

Bok choy, lettuce, spinach—Place a large bowl in the sink. Fill bowl with water. Swish the greens in the water. Individually inspect each leaf for dirt, especially rub the stem and in the creases of each leaf. Set leaves in a colander to drain.

Broccoli, cauliflower—Wash these cruciferous vegetables under running water or swish in a bowl of water. Trim off the tough end of the stem.

Brussels sprouts—Swish brussels sprouts in a bowl of water. When whole brussels sprouts will be served, it is best to trim off the ragged outer leaves. If the brussels spouts will be blended or chopped, trimming off leaves is not so important; just trim off any discolorations. If cooking whole brussels sprouts, put an X-cut in the bottom stem end to help them cook more quickly and evenly.

Celery—Brush celery under running water, along both sides of stems to remove dirt. Trim the ends. Hold the celery at each cut end of a stalk. Bend the stalk backwards so it breaks in the middle exposing the strings that run up the outer side of the stalk. Then, pulling apart with an upwards motion, pull strings off stalk from middle to ends.

Ginger (fresh)—Wash the ginger by rubbing it gingerly under running water. Peel carefully with a peeler or knife. Chop it crosswise to cut through the strings; then chop finely for most uses. Good fresh ginger is very strong and a little will go a long way.

27

Green beans—Swish green beans in a bowl of water. Trim off the stem ends of the green beans.

Herbs (fresh basil, cilantro, mint, and parsley)—When using fresh herbs, wash by swishing herbs in a bowl of cool water. If using herbs for a garnish, you may want to leave a sprig of leaves attached to a short stem. Otherwise, remove the leaves from the stems by plucking. Use the leaves, not the stems. Herbs are generally chopped finely which will distribute their flavor when using them in a recipe.

Mango—Wash the mango under running water. Place the mango on chopping board and hold it carefully on one side. Slice the mango in thirds so the middle third contains the pit. The outer two thirds can be scored (don't cut through the peel) into chunks which will easily cut or scrape from the peel. Peel the center third and cut or scrape remaining fruit from pit.

Mushrooms—I use water to clean, but they are like a sponge so don't soak them. Some people just brush off the dirt with a soft brush. The end of the stem is usually discolored and should be sliced off.

Onion—Wash onion under running water. Remove papery outer layers before chopping. Plan ahead to do the onion quickly and wash up right away if onion makes you cry easily. Onion hints to cry less: keep your face from being directly over the onion, wash onion in cool water, chop onion with the root intact then remove root last.

Potatoes, sweet potatoes, yams, beets, and carrots—Wash: Scrub under water by placing a large bowl in the sink, filling it with water, then scrubbing with a vegetable brush. In lieu of a vegetable brush, a nail brush will work. Soaking loosens the dirt, scrubbing underwater prevents splattering dirt on the wall. Rinse.

Trim: Remove eyes from potatoes. They can be scraped out with the tip of a paring knife. I do not usually peel potatoes because the best nutrients are found at the skin. Trim ends off beets and carrots, peeling is optional. Sweet potatoes and yams can be peeled before or after cooking if the peel does not suit your tastes. If you wait to peel after they are cooked, allow to cool to handle and the peel often comes off with no peeler required, easier than when raw.

Bake: If sweet potatoes, yams, beets, or carrots are baked, they require a baking sheet or aluminum foil under them whereas baking potatoes or other white potatoes do not. Always poke any kind of potato with a fork or knife prior to baking to allow air to escape and prevent explosion as they bake.

Peppers—Rub peppers under running water to clean. Chop peppers open to remove seeds, stem, and insides.

Zucchini—Wash zucchini under running water gently with scrub brush or firmly with the palm of your hand. Trim off both ends.

Some other items that need additional knowledge to prepare:

Dates—These are a dried fruit that do not have to be washed, but wanted to include them in this preparation list because they are usually bought pitted. Even so, the machines may miss a pit occasionally. When using dates, always slice them lengthwise and look for a pit. If the stems are on some of the dates, remove them too.

Olives—These are sold as canned or bottled items and may come with or without pits. Always check for and remove pits when using olives in a recipe.

Tofu—It often comes in blocks packaged in a plastic container with water. They used to be 1 pound. Now 12 or 14 ounces is more common. Take the package to the sink and slice it open around the edge. Drain and rinse the tofu. Store any remaining tofu in a covered container with water covering the tofu. Change the water daily and use within a few days.

General chopping tips:

Always place the vegetable on a cutting board. **Use a sharp knife** because a sharp knife is safer than a dull knife. For any round objects, cut them in half to make flat surfaces. Place the flat surface on the cutting board so the vegetable doesn't roll. This is especially important for hard vegetables such as potatoes, not so important for mushrooms. Keep fingers out of the way. With smaller veggies such as mushrooms, try placing the knife on the object and "bridge" it with thumb and fingers above the knife and onto the ends of the vegetable. Always cut down towards the cutting board.

Shopping tips—When making a **shopping list** from the ingredients in the recipes, generally ignore anything after the "," such as "1 banana, mashed" and "1 large zucchini, chopped" just buy one whole nice yellow banana and one whole big green zucchini. The banana won't be already mashed, nor will you find chopped zucchini in the produce aisle. If you encounter the opportunity to purchase a mashed banana and a chopped zucchini, chances are they are not maintaining their freshness.

Try to enjoy shopping for ingredients that may be new to you. When I was shopping with my friend Steve in a produce aisle, he noticed that we shop differently. "You shop by looking at the vegetables. I read the signs telling me what they are," he commented.

Precision—Amounts in many recipes of this book can be approximate, especially when working with vegetables. Don't stress about whether your head of broccoli will be big enough. Improvise, substitute, or be creative if you forgot to buy an ingredient.

Be **precise when baking**, especially something that will rise or expand such as cakes or cookies. One needs to measure amounts exactly because baking is more of a science. Some things that go into dishes such as cornstarch with liquid should be precise to get the right consistency.

Cooking tips:

Draining—Often the safest way to drain something is to put it in a colander in the sink. Sometimes cracking the lid of a saucepan slightly and pouring liquid into the sink will work. (Hold saucepan and lid in both hands. Oven mitts are good to use if parts of the saucepan are hot.) Draining and saving cooking water from cooked vegetables is the best way to get good vegetable stock. Store the stock in refrigerator after it cools. Use in the following day or two.

Double boiler—Make a double boiler (Chocolate Macadamia Nut Cookies p. 88 and Foxy Fudge p. 157) by placing a small metal mixing bowl or small saucepan on top of a medium saucepan and filling the lower saucepan with an inch or two of water. Be careful not to get burned by rising steam from the boiling water below as you check on the melting of ingredients in the upper saucepan.

Simmer—When cooking on the stove, simmer means to keep liquid bubbling along with only little bubbles after water boils with big bubbles, but reduce heat to low, medium-low, or a combination of the two. The exact temperature of a good simmer depends on stove factors including whether using electric or gas, stove brand, altitude, thickness of saucepan, and temperature of surroundings.

Stove/oven safety—Directions tell you to turn on the stove, but don't tell you to turn it off. Be sure to turn off the stove or oven when finished. When using oven, always use oven mitts to prevent burning your hands. Be careful opening a saucepan that has been cooking; steam under lid can burn if you open towards your face. Keep saucepan handles turned away from the edges of the stove where they can be bumped, but do not put them over other burners.

Timing—Directions typically give you cooking times. Most ovens come with a timer for you to set. A kitchen timer is handy to use for timing because you can take it with you if you need to leave the kitchen. In lieu of a timer, or when cooking more things simultaneously than you have available timers, write down the time something began cooking and remember to check the clock while it cooks.

Vegan Ingredients in These Recipes

Throughout this book the recipes use ingredients that are typically found in most supermarkets today. However, some ingredients may not be familiar to someone who eats a standard American diet. The nonvegans in the following stories asked questions regarding ingredients listed below. Nutritional yeast is probably the hardest to find and may require a trip to a natural foods market.

Legumes and other proteins

Legumes are peas (round), beans (oval or kidney-shaped), and lentils (flattened biconvex). They are a good source of protein and carbohydrates.

Garbanzos—Also known as chickpeas, garbanzos are yellow and larger than a green pea, rich in flavor and nutrition.

Lentils—These small quick-cooking legumes come in a variety of sizes and colors.

Meat analogs—Vegan ground beef substitute and vegan sausage are commercial products made from soy and/or wheat protein prepackaged, ready to heat-and-eat or use as an ingredient.

Soymilk—Milk made from soybeans easily stands in for milk to make vegan recipes.

Tofu—The versatile white cube precipitated from soymilk is bland by itself. It takes on flavors of the other ingredients in a recipe and provides good substance for a meaty texture in a main dish or binding a dessert without eggs.

TVP (textured vegetable protein)—Dehydrated soy protein used as a meat substitute; TVP cooks quickly and absorbs flavor from other ingredients in a recipe.

Nuts, seeds, and oils

Nuts—Cashews, walnuts, hazelnuts (filberts), pecans, macadamia nuts, and many more nuts each have a unique flavor. They can be interchanged in recipes, but it's best to try the ingredient listed the first time you make a recipe.

Tahini—Made from sesame seeds, tahini is similar to a thin nut butter, available roasted (preferred) or raw.

Margarine—Vegan margarine is usually soy oil based. It may contain palm, canola, olive, flax, corn, or other oils. Be sure it does not contain dairy products or hydrogenated oils. Use like butter.

Mayonnaise—Several vegan mayonnaise products are available to substitute for regular mayonnaise. They are often soy based and may require a trip to the health food store if not available at a regular supermarket.

Oils—Corn or other vegetable oils are good for baked desserts. Light olive oil is good for pan-frying vegetables while extra-virgin olive oil is more common in salad dressings.

Vegetables

Vegetables are the most fun to explore early in the dating process. Most people can name at least three vegetables they like, while some can name thirty. The recipes in this book call for vegetables that can be found in almost any supermarket. The confusing or less common ones include:

Bok choy—A type of Chinese cabbage that has dark green leaves with wide white stems.

Brussels sprouts—These look like tiny cabbages with a stronger than cabbage flavor.

Potatoes—**White potatoes** in this book are white "boiling" potatoes, often with a waxy (not waxed) skin. Yukon gold (slightly yellow) or new (small, clean) potatoes can be used for white potatoes. **Russet** or Idaho potatoes are typically larger, dirtier potatoes with a rough skin used for baking. **Sweet potatoes** tend to have yellow insides. **Yams** are easier to find at most supermarkets; they are larger and have orange insides. These recipes use sweet potatoes and yams interchangeably.

Water chestnuts—These crunchy, white spheres are popular in Chinese vegetable dishes. Canned water chestnuts are often found with the international foods.

Vegetables can often be substituted for each other; for instance, dark green leafy vegetables like spinach, kale, collard greens, Swiss chard, and bok choy may vary in taste and cooking time, but should not alter the overall success of a recipe. Broccoli, cauliflower, brussels sprouts, and cabbage can be substituted for each other depending on availability and personal preferences. Many frozen vegetables are also interchangeable.

Fruits

Fruits are terrific for breakfast, snacks, and desserts. They are simple, flavorful, nutritious, and a frequent ingredient in vegan recipes. This book uses common fruits such as apple, mango, banana, and strawberries, and dried fruits such as dates and raisins.

Grains

The grains most people are familiar with are wheat and rice, but there are many other wonderful grains, such as millet, amaranth, and barley. This book uses wheat, rice, quinoa, and oats.

Wheat Flour—When most people think of flour, it is white flour that is usually bleached and lacking in nutrients compared with whole grain flours. **White flour** is milled from only the endosperm part of the wheat. **Whole wheat flour** is ground from the entire wheat berry: the endosperm, bran, and germ. Unless specified, whole wheat flour is usually bread flour, made from hard spring wheat with a high gluten content. **Whole wheat pastry flour** is lighter than bread flour; it is soft wheat, better for pastries and cakes, and more difficult to find. **Unbleached all-purpose flour** is generally a blend of hard and soft white flour used for bread or pastry. It can be substituted for whole wheat flour or whole wheat pastry flour, although it is not as healthful.

Rice—**Brown rice** and **white rice** come from the same plant but brown rice has more vitamins, minerals, and protein because **white rice** has had the bran and germ removed. Brown rice generally takes longer to cook than white rice, but is worth the wait. Different varieties of rice have different flavors. **Basmati** is an aromatic, flavorful long-grain rice from India.

Quinoa—Although grouped with grains, quinoa is an ancient seed high in protein. It can be used like rice but it cooks more quickly. Quinoa should be soaked in water for at least 15 minutes and rinsed in a fine strainer prior to cooking. Quinoa is typically available in white or red.

Oats—Quick oats are most common. Old-fashioned are bigger, heartier, take longer to cook; they give good dimension to oatmeal cookies.

Phyllo dough—Sheets of this paper-thin pastry dough are brushed with oil, layered, and baked to create flaky crusts. Store-bought phyllo is much easier than homemade and vegan whole wheat brands are available.

Sweeteners

The recipes in this book use four kinds of sweeteners: white grape juice, dried fruits (dates or raisins), sugar (usually raw cane sugar crystals), and syrup.

White grape juice—A mild sweetener that also can be offered to dates as non-alcoholic beverage like a mild wine. The sparkling variety is nice to drink, while the regular variety is for recipes or drinking.

Dried fruits are good natural sweeteners. Dates and raisins are used in this book, although you could substitute apricots and figs.

Sugars:

White sugar—Generally made from sugarcane (although it can also come from beets), sugar is refined by extracting molasses.

Raw cane sugar crystals—Large light brown crystals of sugar cane are often called turbinado sugar or evaporated cane juice. This is my preference in recipes. Sometimes the name depends on the size of the crystals. Raw cane sugar is less processed than brown or white sugar, and so is considered better, but still should be used in moderation.

Brown sugar—Brown sugar is not less-refined white sugar; it is white sugar with the molasses added back in. More molasses is added for dark brown sugar.

Confectioners' sugar—Also known as powdered sugar, a finely ground white sugar with cornstarch added. This is a highly processed form of white sugar. It is in one recipe in the book, not encouraged for standard use. Confectioner's sugar can help create a vegan treat similar to a nonvegan version (See Tiramisu p. 153).

Syrups

These liquid sweeteners are listed in descending order of preference for use in recipes; they can be substituted for each other.

Maple syrup—The evaporated sap from the sugar maple tree is delicious sweetener in desserts.

Agave syrup—This liquid from cactus is less flavorful than maple syrup.

Corn syrup—Made from corn, it is often processed with chemicals into high fructose corn syrup for extra sweetness.

Pancake syrup—Colored liquid sugar or corn syrup that could be used if it is the only thing available.

Herbs and seasonings

Herbs and seasonings are used sparingly and amounts can be increased to taste.

Basil—Green fragrant leaves commonly used with tomatoes.

Curry powder—A Indian blend of spices often including: turmeric, coriander, cumin, fenugreek, mustard, and cloves.

Ginger—Three different forms are used in this book. **Fresh ginger** is the stringy root of the ginger plant. It imparts a unique flavor to desserts or vegetable dishes. Ginger can range from mild to hot. **Crystallized ginger** is the consistency of dried fruit such as apricots or dates, but has the spicy bite of fresh ginger and is covered in sugar. **Ground dried ginger** is available in a spice jar or the bulk section of natural food stores.

Italian seasoning—A dry mix of herbs that usually includes thyme, oregano, marjoram, basil, rosemary, and sage.

Poppy seeds—Add a light crunch to desserts or for use as a thickener. Caution: Poppy seeds have been known to give a positive drug test for opiates.

Spearmint—Dry or fresh spearmint leaves can be used to make tea or season vegetables such as potatoes.

Turmeric—Turmeric is a perennial in the ginger family; its rhizomes (underground stems) are dried to make a yellow savory spice used more for color than flavor.

Miscellaneous

Capers—Pickled flower buds used in Mediterranean recipes and found in the international aisle of the supermarket.

Chocolate—Commonly made with milk. However, you can find nondairy dark chocolate chips, chunks, powder, or bars, often on the shelf next to the dairy varieties. Chocolate chunks are similar to chocolate chips, but slightly larger and cube-shape.

Flaxseeds—This good source of omega-3 oil should be ground; use a blender or coffee grinder.

Portobello mushrooms—These large, flat brown mushrooms pack a meaty flavor.

Yeast—Two distinct varieties of yeast, a type of fungus, are used in cooking. **Nutritional yeast** is high in B vitamins, especially B12. It imparts a hint of cheesy flavor to dishes. Active dry **baking yeast** makes bread rise, and must be baked.

Zest—The outermost, colored portion of citrus fruit peels, zest can be peeled or grated. Do not use the bitter white part of the peel.

Vegan Substitutes

How to substitute ingredients as one learns to cook vegan

Meat: Vegans get protein from beans, peas, nuts, and seeds sources. Many commercial imitation meat products, made mostly from wheat or soybeans, re-create the texture and flavor of meat in familiar forms, such as burgers or sausage. Mushrooms also make good non-meat options.

Eggs: Substitution depends on the original purpose of the eggs. Often, such as for pumpkin pie and many cookies, eggs can just be left out. If an egg substitute is desired for binding, use arrowroot starch, potato starch, cornstarch, oat flour, wheat flour, quick oats, mashed potato, or quick-cooking tapioca. Lightness can be created with extra baking yeast or baking soda and by using fruit juice, tomato juice, water or soymilk to replace the liquid from the eggs. Tofu, mashed banana, cooked sweet potato, and ground flaxseeds also find their way into recipes in place of eggs.

Milk: Although soymilk is the easiest to find at most grocery stores, many kinds of milk substitutes are available, including almond milk, rice milk, coconut milk, and hemp milk. As a beverage, they taste different from cow's milk, but they can be used in most recipes just like milk. Chocolate soymilk is a popular, and realistic, copy of chocolate milk.

Yogurt: More brands of soy yogurt are becoming available, some at typical supermarkets, some at health food stores. Soy yogurt is sold in single servings or larger tubs, with the smaller in many fruit flavors. Taste varies with brand.

Cheese: There are a few vegan cheeses commercially available without objectionable ingredients such as casein. There are also many delicious foods that can be used in place of cheese even though they don't imitate it, including hummus, nut butter, and avocados. For those who truly love cheese and want to make vegan versions, buy *The Uncheese Cookbook* by Jo Stepaniak. None of the recipes in *Dating Vegans* require cheese substitutes.

Vegan Substitutes

Ice cream: Often called frozen nondairy dessert, vegan ice cream is readily available in lots of flavors.

Some vegan substitutes are arguably very different. Some are better than the animal product version, some will never match up. New vegan options are becoming widely available.

Being vegan is a delightful journey of compassion. When vegan options are fully explored most people eat a wider variety of healthier foods than when they relied on traditional animal-based fare.

Steve Becker shops for spinach.

Excuse me!

"Excuse me. I need to check that the stars are still shining." Guy ventured out into the cold night mountain air. I thought our vegan dinner date at my cabin was going well and had invited him to stay for breakfast. I was puzzled that he didn't invite me to accompany him for a romantic stroll across the crunchy bright snow.

Upon his return, I inquired of the stars' status and received the following information: "Gaseous balls are burning out there tonight. Thank you for the breakfast invitation but I have to pass." He gave me a hurried goodnight, said he looked forward to seeing me soon, and disappeared down the moonlit path again. I was more stumped than a log in a woodpile.

When a nonvegan eats with a vegan, emotional and physical changes may be experienced. This is normal. Symptoms may include giddiness, increased energy, and flatulence. With an increase in plant-source fiber, there may be noticeable adjustments in the digestion process.

Give the new relationship with a person and foods time to come to fruition. Vegan protein is commonly derived from nuts and from beans, which are well known for their aerial attacks while one adjusts to their consumption. Introduce new vegan foods gradually. The nonvegan can try eating some vegan foods when not with the vegan. Both partners need to be patient and understanding during the early relationship with regards to potential for spontaneous embarrassment.

"I remember that evening. Your cooking was great." Guy said when I read this to him. "If I could go back in time, I would risk spending the night."

Stories and Recipes

from Dates with Meat-Eating Men

The meet and potatoes of the book

Mighty Athlete Afraid of Rabbit Food

Paul Bergman

Paul Bergman was finishing his master's degree in organizational leadership at Mercyhurst College, where he worked as assistant wrestling coach. His final day in Erie, Pennsylvania, we had our first dinner. Paul and I had been friends for over a year, as he taught me to wrestle. He never wanted anything in return for his patient coaching, yet he appreciated vegan cupcakes and cookies mysteriously appearing on his desk. Paul, a typical meat eater, had never socialized with a vegan and never gave much thought to his food choices prior to our discussion. He is an independent thinker with mainstream taste buds, and his witty, well-educated, open mind made him a good challenge for my new recipe project. I decided to keep the menu as conventional as possible.

Paul's expectations of a vegan meal consisted of a fresh salad with dandelions. I resisted the urge to go foraging in his front yard for my missing ingredient. "The salad was good, really good," Paul said of the assorted baby lettuces, tomatoes, baby carrots, cucumber, and raisins that I served him. I had tossed it with a store-bought sesame-shiitake dressing. Store-bought dressing and other convenience foods can help nonvegans see veganism as a viable option. I created Paul's Portobello Potatoes for the main course, using his favorite vegetables. "The only thing missing was a side steak, but I wouldn't have had room for that," he said. "The potato was loaded!"

We discussed veganism. He was aware vegans do not use eggs, milk, and other animal products. "Wait, so the ice cream we will be having doesn't have any milk? Is it tofu?" Paul expected the nondairy vanilla ice cream dished onto the Takedown Chocolate Brownies to be a weird concoction. "The first bite was different. After that, it tasted the way any other ice cream, strawberries, and brownie would taste. Good to the last bite!"

Mighty Athlete Afraid of Rabbit Food

Would a large, athletic guy with a healthy appetite eat vegan dinner again? "Yes, definitely!" Would this experience influence him? "Fatty meats probably aren't the best thing. I thought more about healthy eating with vegan-style food tonight. Psychologically, I'm feeling really healthy right now. Physically, I'm a little full."

Secretly, I beamed with pride that I had exceeded his expectations while satisfying his appetite. And I managed to eat my whole dinner without any lettuce flying out my nose during our vegan-issues conversation, which was riddled with Paul's inadvertent, stoic humor. Paul had asked how many vegans there are in the United States. I know there are more vegans now than when I was a child; but he hungered for specifics, and my answer left him unsatisfied. We looked on the Vegetarian Resource Group website (vrg.org) and deduced that at least one percent of the population considers themselves vegan, and the number is increasing. Over three million vegans in this country, and I am the only one who has had the pleasure of sharing dinner with Paul.

Vegans date nonvegans because there are 99 times more people from which to choose. It helps to keep in mind that anyone can be a vegan, but 99 percent of the population has not made that decision yet. Dating should be sharing enjoyable picnics at the rest stops on the journey of life, not a goal to detour someone else. Dating can be fun and educational.

The American Vegan Society website (americanvegan.org) provides a basic definition of veganism that Paul found helpful. Paul had not considered that some things, such as honey, are not vegan. This inspired him to reflect that if he were unsure whether an item was acceptable, he would respectfully ask a vegan. "Meat eaters eat a lot of foods that vegans eat," he commented. "Food is just a small part of life. There are more difficult situations to resolve than how to eat a meal together." After our successful dinner, Paul expressed interest in trying a few "strange" vegan foods, such as more exotic whole grains. We decided to do dinner again the next time he is in town.

Paul might always say "I like meat" defensively, with his dimpled smirk, or he might continue to learn about veganism. Either way, we had a wonderful evening and a positive social interaction between a vegan and a nonvegan. Thank you, Paul.

Paul's Portobello Potatoes

Yield: 3 big manly servings

When I asked Paul what his three favorite vegetables were, he replied, "Salsa."

I wondered if he came from the kind of background where ketchup is considered a vegetable, but I gave him the benefit of the doubt. "Besides salsa, what vegetables do you like?"

"Potatoes, corn, and mushrooms," he replied. Paul's Portobello Potatoes uses all three of his favorite vegetables, and they're even topped with salsa!

3 large russet potatoes (preferably organic), scrubbed but not
  peeled
3 Tablespoons plain soymilk
3 Tablespoons olive oil
1/2 large red bell pepper, chopped, or 1/2 cup frozen chopped
  red bell pepper
6 baby (or 1 large) portobello mushrooms with stems, chopped
1/2 cup corn kernels
1/4 teaspoon salt (optional)
1 teaspoon dried spearmint or basil
6 Tablespoons salsa

Preheat the oven to 350 degrees F.

Poke a few holes in the potatoes with a fork. Arrange the potatoes directly on the center rack of the oven. Bake for 1 hour, or until a knife can slide in easily. Let the potatoes cool until they can be easily handled.

Slice each potato top open lengthwise. With a spoon, scoop the potato flesh into a large bowl, leaving about 1/4 inch of flesh attached to the skins so they will hold their shape.

Add the soymilk and oil to bowl of potatoes and mash together with a fork. Add the pepper, mushrooms, corn, and salt, if using, to the potatoes. Mix well. Crush the spearmint with your fingers directly over the potato mixture and mix until evenly distributed.

Carefully stuff the potato skins with the vegetable mixture, mounding it slightly. Arrange the potatoes in a baking dish. Bake for 20 minutes. Top each potato with 2 tablespoons of salsa before serving.

Takedown Chocolate Brownies

Yield: 12 brownies

Paul disclosed his love of chocolate brownies and enjoyed his role as official taste tester for my new recipe. Although he was quite pleased with the third version of the recipe, he encouraged further changes. I played his game for five more batches before attaining perfection and he agreed to join me for a complete meal. These brownies are especially good served with vanilla nondairy ice cream and strawberries.

1 large sweet potato or medium yam, chopped
1 cup vanilla (or plain) soymilk
1/4 cup vegetable oil
1 1/2 cups raw cane sugar crystals
1 1/2 cups unsweetened cocoa powder
2/3 cup whole wheat pastry flour
1/4 teaspoon baking soda
3/4 cup vegan chocolate chips

Preheat the oven to 350 degrees F. Lightly oil a 9 x 13-inch baking pan.

Put the sweet potato in a medium saucepan, add 1 cup water, and bring to a boil over high heat. Reduce the heat to simmer for 30 minutes, or until the sweet potato is tender and a knife can slide in easily. Drain and cool.

Meanwhile, combine the sugar, cocoa powder, flour, and baking soda in a large bowl. Scoop the sweet potato flesh from the skin into a medium bowl, and mash it. Add the soymilk and oil and mix well.

Add the sweet potato mixture to the cocoa mixture and stir until evenly combined. Fold in the chocolate chips. Pour into the prepared baking pan. Bake for 35 minutes, or until a toothpick inserted about 1 inch from the edge comes out clean. Cool, cut into approximately 3-inch square brownies, and serve.

Paul Bergman

Meat-Eater Dances into Cooking Vegan Dinners
Hank Hawkins

Hank and I met in the summer at a contra dance. We had both arrived during a dance and were waiting for the next one to begin.

"Hi, I'm Hank."

"I have a truck named Hank," I said.

"Then we must dance!" It was a great way to start a relationship.

One particular evening, Hank and I decided to plant a small garden, eat dinner, and then cruise Chautauqua Lake in his boat. After the cruise, we enjoyed just sitting in the boat, watching the sunset, without the motor competing for conversation or sucking gas.

While gardening, I doodled on large wooden stakes. Each stake had a drawing of the plant on one side and a drawing of the harvestable vegetable on the other side, along with the name of the plant. "The stakes are fun and provide idiot-proof gardening!" Hank commented.

We made Lentil Garden Stew with ingredients from the store and fantasized about our garden's produce. Fresh Italian bread and vegan margarine complemented the stew. In order to enjoy more date time, I had made Pineapple Upside-Down Cake the day before, and chilled.

Hank has since become a competent cook of simple vegan dinners. One of his best menus is a fresh fruit appetizer (or dessert), Hank's Stir-Fried Veggies, refried beans (which he is careful to purchase without lard or other nonvegan ingredients), and warm tortillas or tortilla chips. Another favorite meal is Pasta with Garden Vegetable Sauce, Festive Garlic-Free Bread, and store-bought vegan lemon-vanilla cookies.

One sunny, late-summer afternoon, Hank and I sat on his porch. A chilly wind hinted that fall was coming soon to western New York. I had gotten a new job and would be moving to Columbus,

Ohio. We decided to celebrate with dinner together and catch some live music at the town square.

Hank created the innovative and incredible "Chocolate" Zucchini, made with bountiful garden squash and pumpernickel bread crumbs. While the "Chocolate" Zucchini baked, Hank shucked and steamed corn on the cob. Since the oven was already on, he made a batch of Double Italian Bread .

Hank gave me a slice of watermelon as an appetizer and told me to relax while he cooked. I relaxed five minutes before I got the urge to create Sweet Zucchini Pie, which will satisfy the sweetest sweet tooth. Relishing each bite, we looked up at the quince tree and wondered how a pie using quince would taste. Quince Pie was quickly determined to be delicious too.

Hank and I have determined we are at different stages in our lives so we date other people, but remain great friends. I will never forget the time Hank told me, "So, I was on this date, and she was talking about beef or chicken. I couldn't believe we were discussing beef or chicken. I was so bored. You've spoiled me for dating other women!" What Hank meant was that he had been hanging out with a vegan friend who had influenced him to think about his food choices, inspired intelligent conversation on a variety of topics, and taught him how to cook a little. That was Hank's way of saying "Thank you." (Hank's photo p. 106)

Lentil Garden Stew

Yield: 4 servings

Hank said, "The lentil base melds the vegetable flavors nicely. I didn't know what lentils were before this. They taste great, and I learned they are like a bean." Lentils are high in protein and give substance to a stew. Unlike other dried beans, they don't require advance planning, as they can cook with the vegetables. For true garden stew, alter the ingredients in late summer to use garden vegetables including kale, bell peppers, tomatoes, and zucchini.

1 cup dried green-brown lentils, picked through and rinsed
3 cups water
1 onion, chopped
1 carrot, chopped
1 white potato, chopped
1 small head broccoli, coarsely chopped
1/2 small head cauliflower, coarsely chopped

Place the lentils in a large saucepan. Add the water and bring to a boil over high heat. Add the onion, carrot, and potato to the lentils and return to a boil. Cover and reduce heat to simmer for 20 minutes.

Add the broccoli and cauliflower to the lentils. Replace the lid and continue cooking for 20 to 30 minutes, or until the lentils and vegetables are tender.

Hank's Stir-Fried Veggies

Yield: 4 servings

Here is a simple main or side dish. Any garden-fresh vegetables can inspire variations.

2 Tablespoons olive oil
1 large carrot, very thinly sliced on the diagonal
1 small head broccoli, cut into bite-size florets
1 zucchini, diced
1/2 green bell pepper, diced
10 small portobello or white button mushrooms (8 ounces),
   sliced

Heat the oil in a large skillet or wok over medium-high heat. Add the carrot and cook for 3 minutes, stirring frequently. Add the broccoli, zucchini and green pepper, and stir. Add the mushrooms. Stir occasionally. Cook approximately 10 minutes total or until all of the vegetables are cooked to your liking.

Pasta with Garden Vegetable Sauce: Yield: 4 to 6 servings. Cook 1 pound of your favorite pasta in boiling water according to the package directions. Add 1 jar (24–26 ounces) of marinara sauce to Hank's Stir-Fried Veggies. Drain the pasta well and ladle the sauce on top.

Festive Garlic-Free Bread

Yield: 6 pieces

This is a great alternative to garlic bread. It leaves no garlic breath to spoil a kiss!

6 slices Italian bread
6 teaspoons vegan margarine
1 1/2 teaspoons nutritional yeast flakes
3/4 teaspoon paprika
3/4 teaspoon rosemary
1/2 teaspoon sage
1/4 teaspoon salt (optional)

Preheat the oven to 350 degrees F.

Lightly spread each bread slice with 1 teaspoon of the margarine. Arrange the slices on a baking sheet, margarine-side up. Sprinkle the bread with the nutritional yeast, paprika, rosemary, sage, and salt, if using. Bake for 5 to 8 minutes, or until lightly toasted.

Note: Herb amounts are approximate. It is easier to sprinkle them directly from their jars if they have shaker tops.

Double-Italian Bread: Replace the nutritional yeast, paprika, rosemary, and sage with 2 teaspoons Italian seasoning.

Pineapple Upside-Down Cake

Yield: 8 servings

"Pineapple upside-down cake is my favorite dessert. I didn't notice any difference in taste, consistency, or texture—I couldn't tell that it was vegan," Hank said. "The syrupy pineapple and cake were perfect."

Although this looks like a long list of ingredients and instructions compared with most recipes I make, it is not difficult. Friends say it's worth the effort!

8 slices (rings) fresh or canned pineapple, core removed
8 pitted cherries (see note)
1 3/4 cups raw cane sugar crystals
3 Tablespoons vegan margarine
1/2 lemon (preferably organic), scrubbed
8 ounces firm tofu, rinsed and drained
3/4 cup white grape juice
1 Tablespoon vanilla extract
1 cup whole wheat bread flour
1 cup whole wheat pastry flour
1 Tablespoon poppy seeds
1 1/2 teaspoons baking soda

Preheat the oven to 350 degrees F.

Melt the margarine in a small saucepan over low heat. Remove from the heat and stir in 1/4 cup of the sugar. Spread the margarine mixture over the bottom of a 9 x 13-inch baking pan baking pan. Arrange the pineapple slices over the margarine mixture in a single layer. Place one cherry in the center of each pineapple slice.

Peel 1 tablespoon of zest from the lemon (use only the top yellow layer of the peel). Squeeze 1 1/2 teaspoons of juice from the lemon. Put the lemon zest and juice in a blender. Crumble the tofu and put it in the blender. Add the remaining 1 1/2 cups of sugar, grape juice, and vanilla. Process until completely smooth.

Combine the bread flour, pastry flour, poppy seeds, and baking soda in a large mixing bowl. Add the tofu mixture and stir until well mixed. Carefully pour over the pineapple in the baking pan, taking care not to disrupt the pineapple and cherries.

Bake for about 40 minutes, or until a toothpick inserted in the center of the cake comes out clean. Slide a knife around the edge of the cake between the cake and the pan. While the cake is still hot, carefully place a large platter or baking sheet over the pan and flip the cake upside down (so the pineapple is on the top). Carefully remove the baking pan by lifting it straight up. Cool completely before serving. Goes great with vegan vanilla ice cream.

Note: Traditionally, one maraschino cherry is placed in the center of each pineapple slice where the core was removed. However, maraschino cherries typically are packed with chemicals, dyes, and lots of sugar. If you prefer, pitted fresh bing cherries may be used as a garnish after baking so as not to discolor the cake.

"Chocolate" Zucchini

Yield: 4 servings

These zucchini slices look like they were playing in decadent chocolate-muffin crumbs, and they will almost fool your taste buds too. Despite their disguise, they are a savory delight.

3 slices pumpernickel bread
2 Tablespoons soy sauce
1 1/2 Tablespoons olive oil
1 pound (3 small or 1 large) zucchini, sliced into 3/8-inch-thick rounds

Preheat the oven to 350 degrees F.

Place the bread in blender, 1 piece at a time, and process it into crumbs. Transfer the crumbs to a plate.

Place the soy sauce and oil in a small flat dish. Beat together with a whisk or fork.

Dip each slice of zucchini in the soy sauce mixture. Then dredge it in the bread crumbs, turning it over to coat both sides, and pressing it with your fingers to help the crumbs adhere. Arrange the breaded zucchini on a baking sheet. Bake for 30 minutes. Serve hot.

Sweet Zucchini Pie

Yield: 8 servings

This is a fun way to serve abundant summer garden squash.

1 (9-inch) graham-cracker pie crust, store-bought
  or see page 78
1/2 cup raw cane sugar crystals
2 Tablespoons whole wheat pastry flour
2 Tablespoons cornstarch
1 teaspoon ground cinnamon
1/2 teaspoon ground ginger
1 large zucchini, chopped (about 3 cups)
10 pitted dates, chopped

Preheat the oven to 350 degrees F. Bake the crust for 8 minutes.

Combine the sugar, flour, cornstarch, cinnamon, and ginger in a large mixing bowl. Add the zucchini and dates and mix until evenly distributed. Spoon the filling into the crust. Bake for 45 minutes or until zucchini is tender. Remove from the oven and gently pack down the filling with a fork. Return to the oven and bake 20 minutes longer for filling to meld. Serve warm or thoroughly chilled.

Quince Pie: Replace the zucchini with an equal amount of chopped quince or sour apples.

"Beeting" Vegan Misconceptions
Philip Spinks

Philip Spinks lights up my life. He is the man I will marry, according to our mutual friend Alex, who coordinated our blind-date introduction. I spotted Philip right away at Alex's party; he captured my attention with his tall, athletic body; short light blond hair; and mysterious, elfin grin. Philip is an electrician at the local power plant, so technically he lights up the life of every woman in the area.

One of Philip's favorite vegetables is green beans, which I forgot to purchase for our date. Looking in my fridge, I found zucchini and a green bell pepper. I sliced them into long, thin lengths, the size of green beans, steamed them, and served him "green beans" with a smirk.

"They don't look like the green beans in my garden," Philip astutely observed. We agreed that if we closed our eyes while eating zucchini "green beans," they tasted like the real thing.

Philip had never eaten beets and trusted me to make his first experience pleasurable. Remembering we both like sweet potatoes, the combination became the root of Roasted Vegetables. Mash-Mix Hummus and toasted pita bread rounded out our meal together. Second helpings allowed us to save dessert for a later treat.

When I had confirmed our date plans, I told Philip to bring jeans and a change of clothes, as our excursion might include thorns and a motorcycle. We wandered the woods surrounding my cabin, gathering a few blackberries and raspberries. Perfect motorcycle weather beckoned us to ride to a blueberry stand for a purchase. As the wind flapped our shirts wherever our bodies were not pressed together, Philip noticed dark clouds forming over Lake Erie.

Losing the race with an oncoming rainstorm, we stopped at the store for a pint of vegan ice cream. Philip quickly chose nondairy chocolate, as the air-conditioned store and its freezer section chilled our wet attire. We returned to my cabin, which was warm and dry, as were our change of clothes. We set about making dessert together, putting berries and heaping generous scoops of ice cream into bowls. I stuffed cashews into pitted dates and placed them alongside the ice cream. He topped each serving with walnuts and crystallized ginger.

Then I lured Philip into my loft with the promise that it was better for conversation. We got close and comfortable and . . . played Scrabble. As we played, we talked about food.

A typical meal for Philip could range from a bowl of cereal to meat on the grill. I asked him if he knew the definitions of "vegetarian" and "vegan," and his response was fairly accurate. "A vegetarian is someone who does not eat meat, and a vegan is a vegetarian who does not use dairy."

Phillip grew up working his parents' dairy farm. He asked why I am vegan, so I explained that my parents were vegan and that it made sense to me from an early age to not eat animals. When he asked why my parents had chosen to be vegan, I told him about their vegetarian upbringing and described my Dad's tour of a slaughterhouse and his subsequent vow to not take a day off from work until every slaughterhouse is closed. All four of my grandparents were vegetarian, but I confessed that I would have to phone my relatives to find out their exact reasons. My heritage is so different from his that he nodded his interest but would let the information digest as we focused on the game.

I was getting lucky while Philip was scoring. When he announced our points, I was usually on top. Near the end of our third and final game he put his "MEAT" on the board. I teased, "Ugh, now you just had to go and put 'MEAT' on the table."

"No. The 'M' is still a blank tile from your 'MOUTH.' So I just score 'E-A-T' and that's okay. We can 'EAT' together."

(Philip's photo p. 99)

Roasted Vegetables

Yield: 4 servings

"Beets taste better than I expected. I might even eat them again some day," declared Philip, the sweet potato lover.

1 large sweet potato or medium yam, cut in 1-inch cubes
1 beet, cut in 1-inch cubes
1 Tablespoon olive oil
1 Tablespoon soy sauce
1 Tablespoon nutritional yeast
1 teaspoon curry powder
1 teaspoon dried oregano
1 teaspoon paprika
1 teaspoon dried dill weed
1/4 teaspoon ground ginger
1 small zucchini, chopped
4 large white button mushrooms, chopped
1 Tablespoon cornstarch

Preheat the oven to 350 degrees F. Place the sweet potato and beet in a 4 x 9-inch loaf pan. Add the oil and soy sauce and mix until the vegetables are evenly coated.

Combine the nutritional yeast, curry powder, oregano, paprika, dill weed, and ginger in a small bowl. Sprinkle half of this seasoning mixture over the sweet potato and beet. Mix until evenly distributed. Bake for 45 minutes.

Put the zucchini and mushrooms in a bowl. Stir the cornstarch into the remaining seasoning mixture. Sprinkle over the zucchini and mushrooms and toss until evenly distributed.

After the sweet potato and beet have baked for 45 minutes, add the zucchini mixture to the pan. Bake for 45 minutes longer, or until a knife can slide easily into any vegetable, and serve.

Mash-Mix Hummus

Yield: 2 cups

I made hummus without the blender. The mashed garbanzos provided great texture. Philip and I played "yes, no, or maybe" with my spices to determine the flavor. After a taste test he said, "Mmm. Reminds me of tuna."

I love having nonvegan dates help me cook. I can honestly say tuna is one of the things I will never eat, not even one stinkin' bite for "research." I would never have equated hummus on pita with a tuna fish salad sandwich.

1 can (15 ounces) garbanzos (chick peas)
2 Tablespoons olive oil
1 Tablespoon roasted sesame tahini
1 Tablespoon lime juice or lemon juice
1 teaspoon dried dill (2 teaspoons fresh dill, finely chopped)
1 teaspoon dried parsley (2 teaspoons fresh parsley, chopped)
1/4 teaspoon ground celery seed
1/8 teaspoon salt (optional)
1/8 teaspoon black pepper (optional)

Drain the garbanzos and put them in a large mixing bowl. Mash the garbanzos, leaving a few lumps for a "tuna" consistency. Add the oil, tahini, and lime juice to the garbanzos and mix well. Add the dill, parsley, celery seed. Add the salt and pepper, if using. Mix well. Serve as a sandwich spread or as a dip.

Creamy Mash-Mix Hummus: Substitute canned great northern beans for the garbanzos. The result is surprisingly creamy hummus.

Philip's Blue Chocolate Dessert

Yield: 2 servings, plus a bit more to share

Philip likes all kinds of dessert and likes to make desserts. I impressed him with how easy it is to make a delicious vegan dessert. Berry season inspired this tasty concoction, which can be a great light summer meal by itself. "I never had stuffed dates before. They were very good. I didn't expect nondairy ice cream to be as good as it was. I never would have tried to put blueberries and chocolate together, but you can't go wrong with chocolate," commented Philip. "The ginger was good too. Now I know why ginger ale tastes like it does and not like beer."

1 pint (2 cups) fresh summer berries (blueberries, blackberries, raspberries)
1 pint vegan chocolate ice cream
6 pitted dates
6 whole raw cashews
6 small pieces crystallized ginger, chopped
6 walnut halves, chopped

Place 3/4 cup of the berries in each of two bowls. Put two or three scoops of ice cream in each bowl, leaving almost a serving in the container. Slice each date lengthwise, insert a cashew, and close. Place the stuffed dates next to the ice cream. Sprinkle the ginger and walnuts on top of the ice cream.

Eat before it melts. When the bowls are empty, remember there is a little bit left of the berries and ice cream to share. Sometimes a dessert shared in one dish tastes better between two!

How Much Meat Can I Stomach?

Dave Nagel

Lula, a retired dairy cow, was slaughtered and butchered into 443 pounds of hamburger, steaks, and roasts—enough meat to supply a man for three years. Why did he not buy three years' worth of vegetables, beans, or nuts? I respect that each person has the right to make his or her own decisions. If those decisions hurt others (such as Lula), does the person still have just as much right of choice? Could I date a man who makes this type of choice? Is it better than dating the man who does not think about the choice and robotically picks up the meat package from the store shelf every week? Are people addicted to meat?

Meanwhile, I should explain that I am addicted to accomplishment. My favorite thing to do with someone is make something. We could be making a piece of furniture, a quilt, a stone patio, or a recipe. As this is a dating story, maybe I should include making love?

The man in this story is my friend, Dave Nagel. I do not make love with Dave, opting for making chimneys instead. We make good conversation with humorous sexual undertones as I help him with occasional masonry projects. One afternoon as Dave devoured one of my cashew butter and strawberry jelly sandwiches on whole wheat bread, I thought it would be fun to cook a vegan meal for him.

Dave's three favorite vegetables are "Potatoes, all squashes, cabbage, cauliflower, broccoli, brussels sprouts, onion, radish, lettuce." I laughed at how he is good at counting bricks, not so good at counting three vegetables, while I scribbled them down. "I never had a veggie I didn't like," he said. As I was wondering what culinary challenge I could find in his vegetable list he added, "I've never had an eggplant."

"Promise me you won't eat an eggplant until we have dinner," I requested.

"You want me to remain an eggplant virgin until you can have your way with me," he grinned in agreement. The next week, in the midst of restoring the mortar on a stone chimney originally built in 1875, Dave savored a picnic lunch including a sandwich I made using Randall's Baked Eggplant (p. 168).

I am the only vegetarian Dave knows. I asked, "Do you know what a vegan is?"

"Vegan? Never heard of it."

"Do you want to take a guess?"

"Vegan. Hmmm," Dave thought for a moment. "Someone who never has sex?"

We chortled and I told him the definition of vegan before admitting to being a vegan. We bantered about sex, meat, and dating. Dave usually cooks meat dishes: goulash, chicken casserole with rice, steaks, slow cooked pot roast, baked ham, and hamburger.

"Ever make anything without meat?" I asked.

"No, I like sex. Couldn't be a vegan."

Sometimes it is better to pretend to lose an argument and enjoy a laugh together.

Dave's house is a raised ranch in the rolling country hills of western New York. A stone's throw behind the house sits the chicken coop inhabited by a rooster, a hen, and two little chicks. Dave is also raising a pig named Sue who will become Lula's roommate in the freezer as ham, bacon, and pork chops. I asked if the chickens become casserole.

"I let them grow. I let them be chickens. They run around in the yard. They eat insects, peck, scratch, and do what chickens do. I don't feel like killing or eating them. The raccoons kill some. They have a hard enough time without me killing them." Sometimes

Dave collects the eggs to eat; sometimes he lets the hen sit on the eggs to hatch.

I didn't understand the distinction he made between killing the pig and keeping the chickens, deducing he makes chicken casserole with store-bought chickens. "Pig is for meat, chickens are to watch." Dave explained the tranquil feeling he has watching them, "Chickens are part of the folklore of the property. The rooster crows in the morning, starting about 3:30. I'm a country boy out here in the sticks."

Next I will have to make him a beans-and-rice-without-chicken casserole. I continued to ponder my dating questions: Is it better dating a man who does not think about his food choices or one who does? Could I love a man who chooses to kill animals?

Extra Tasty Mashed Potatoes

Yield: 8 cups

This terrific alternative to the classic mashed potatoes with peas on the side eliminates chasing peas around the plate. Leftovers, if there are any, are good in other recipes such as Potato Balls, Dave's Stuffed Mushrooms, or they can be fried for breakfast.

6 large white potatoes, chopped
1 sweet potato, peeled and chopped
1 small yellow onion, chopped
8 ounces white or portobello mushrooms, sliced
2 Tablespoons vegan margarine
1 1/2 cups frozen peas
1/2 cup plain soymilk
1/2 teaspoon salt (optional)

Place the white potatoes and sweet potato in a large saucepan, add 2 cups water, and bring to a boil over high heat. Cover, reduce the heat, and simmer for 30 minutes, or until the potatoes are tender and a knife can slide in easily. Drain the potatoes, saving the cooking water, and place the potatoes in a large bowl.

Place the margarine in a large skillet over medium-high heat. (These steps could be done while the potatoes are cooking.) Add the onion and cook, stirring occasionally, 5 minutes, or until the onion begins to become translucent. Add the mushrooms and peas to the pan; stir and cook 2 additional minutes.

Mash the potatoes. Add the soymilk and mix with the potatoes. Gradually add some of the reserved cooking water if creamier mashed potatoes are desired. Add the fried vegetables and salt, if using, mix well, and serve.

Potato Balls

Yield: 16 (2-bite) balls

As I ate a scrumptious dinner including Extra Tasty Mashed Potatoes alone, I wished I had invited Dave. I solved my leftovers problem the next day by surprising Dave with a picnic lunch. Mashed potatoes became Potato Balls."These are perfect, excellent. I like the peas and onions together," he said.

2 cups potato chips, wavy variety
1 cup Extra Tasty Mashed Potatoes, chilled

Smash the potato chips until you have 1 cup of crumbs (a small fist in the measuring cup works well or use a spoon), and spread them on a large plate. Scoop a tablespoon-sized portion of mashed potato and roll between your hands to form a ball. Roll the ball in the chips until coated and then gently roll the ball between your hands again to be sure the chips are stuck to the potatoes. Place the ball on a plate and repeat with the remaining mashed potatoes and crushed chips. Serve.

Dave's Stuffed Mushrooms

Yield: 6 servings

"I love the stuffed mushrooms, everything about them: the texture and flavor. They're great," Dave commented.

6 large stuffable mushrooms (extra large white button
  mushrooms or medium portobello mushrooms)
1 cup Extra Tasty Mashed Potatoes, chilled
1/8 teaspoon cayenne pepper
2 Tablespoons ground hazelnuts (filberts)
1 teaspoon paprika

Preheat the oven to 375 degrees F. Lightly oil a baking dish large enough for all the mushrooms side-by-side.

Place the mushroom caps with their rounded surface down in the baking dish. Spoon the potatoes into the mushroom caps, forming shapely mounds. Sprinkle the top of the potatoes with the cayenne, then top with the nuts and paprika.

Bake for 20 minutes, or until the mushrooms soften and a knife can slide in easily. Serve.

Oatmeal Raisin Cookies

Yield: 6 dozen cookies

Six dozen sounds like a lot, but they disappear quickly and can be frozen.

1 cup vegan margarine
1 cup maple syrup
1 cup orange juice
2 Tablespoons vanilla extract
3 3/4 cups whole wheat pastry flour
1 1/2 cups raw cane sugar crystals
1 teaspoon ground cinnamon
1/4 teaspoon baking soda

1 banana, mashed
3 cups old-fashioned oats (see note)
3 cups raisins

Preheat the oven to 350 degrees F. Line two large baking sheets with parchment paper.

Melt the margarine in a small saucepan over low heat. Remove from the heat and stir in the maple syrup, orange juice, and vanilla. Mix the flour, sugar, cinnamon, and baking soda in a large bowl. Pour the wet mixture into the dry mixture making sure to smash out the lumps. Stir in the mashed banana. Add the oats and raisins and mix. (The banana, oats, and raisins will give the dough desirable lumps.) Let the dough sit for 5 minutes to allow the oats to absorb moisture.

Drop the dough by heaping teaspoons onto a prepared baking sheet, allowing 1 inch between the cookies. Repeat the process on the second baking sheet.

Bake for 15 to 20 minutes or until the cookies are lightly browned on the bottom and soft but not wet on top. Remove baking sheets from oven and let cookies cool 5 minutes on the baking sheets; then transfer the cookies to wire racks. Repeat forming and baking cookies with remaining dough on the re-useable parchment. The cookies can be enjoyed warm or cool.

Note: Quick oats can be used instead of old-fashioned. Cookies will be less chewy.

Chocolate Chip Oatmeal Raisin Cookies: Reduce the amount of raisins to 2 cups and add 2 cups chocolate chips.

Ninja Brussels Sprouts
Brad Holdren

Brad Holdren is a rowing coach whose secret lifelong ambition is to become Homer Simpson. However, Brad is well educated and witty while Homer is wonderfully unburdened with knowledge. I invited Brad/Homer to visit me in Columbus for a date. Brad said if I could come up with a way to make brussels sprouts palatable, I would be a miracle worker. My devious mind eagerly accepted the challenge.

Brad arrived late due to an emergency meeting at work—a donut shortage or something. Brad loved the Mushroom Soup and Veggie Pie. I disclosed their high brussels sprout content halfway through the lunch.

For dinner Brad and I invented Brussels Sprout Curry with Red Quinoa. With my last hurrah, Apple Mango Pie, I tried to keep a poker face as I thought about specks of four large brussels sprouts lurking in the sauce particles. Brad took the first bite, "This is scrumptious, fantastic!"

"How do you like the brussels sprouts in this?"

"There are NOT brussels spouts in this!"

"Yes, there are!" I nodded emphatically.

"No, people wouldn't do that to a pie," Brad insisted.

"Maybe I'm not human."

"If you did, there's a special place in hell waiting for you. But the pie's still good. It is transcendent, like when Homer tasted something incredible off his shirt and Lisa was typing his food review."

I got Brad to eat four dishes with brussels sprouts.

"D'oh!!!"

Brad and I either met at a rowing conference or a regatta; which one, neither of us remembers. When rowing coaches have a date, they explore rowing venues. Between meals we hiked at my job-site, The Ohio State University, with his two dogs. Brad mused about enjoying the huge campus, "Ohio State is a bit disturbing because I grew up as a Michigan fan. I realize I'm more of an Ohio State fan now. I can say that. I won't get my house egged because only vegans will read this and they don't own eggs."

I asked if he knows what a vegan is. He replied, "A problem on the team that you have to deal with when you are planning team trips and dinners."

"So you have had vegans on your rowing team?"

Brad's crew averages one or two vegans or vegetarians every year. "It's getting to the point where it's rarer to not have a vegan on the team than it is to have one. It's still rare to have more than one. We have one vegetarian right now. We all dance around her with turkey legs at every opportunity."

"I tease the vegans and tell them we will be able to strip the bark off a tree outside the restaurant for them. It opens up a line of discussion between them and the other team members. I emphasize the stupid stereotypes in order to get the discussion started. I've asked if they've chosen to be vegan because they love animals or because they hate plants. And then I break out one of my favorite Homer Simpson quotes. Homer asks his daughter Lisa, 'Are you saying you're never going to eat any animal again? What about bacon?' 'No,' says Lisa. 'Ham?' 'No!' 'Pork chops?' Lisa replies, 'Dad those all come from the same animal!' 'Heh, heh, heh. Ooh, yeah, right, Lisa. A wonderful, magical animal.' It helps to have Homer's imagination balloon floating above his head with the animal. He's so dumb he doesn't know they are all pig."

Mushroom Soup

Yield: 8 cups

Challenged to find ways to serve brussels sprouts, I created this easy soup. I kept the beautiful light green color, while mushrooms served as a good distraction. This soup goes well with and is an ingredient in Veggie Pie. Brad serves this soup with a garnish of fresh chopped dill and a dill pickle. I prefer crackers.

"I love soup! All soups. You don't get a body like mine being picky about food." I informed Brad the color came from puree of brussels sprouts. He choked, gasped, and said, "I liked it anyway because it was soup."

12 brussels sprouts
1 large white potato, cut into 1-inch chunks
2 celery stalks, chopped
1/8 head green cabbage, chopped
4 1/2 cups water or vegetable stock
8 ounces white button or portobello mushrooms, sliced

Place the potato, celery, cabbage, and brussels sprouts in a large saucepan, add 3 cups of the water, and bring to a boil over high heat. Cover, reduce the heat, and simmer about 30 minutes or until the potato is tender and a knife can slide in easily.

Allow the cooked vegetables to cool enough to handle. Transfer all the vegetables with some of the cooking water from the saucepan to a blender. Process the soup until smooth; additional water may be used to help it blend. Return the soup to the saucepan over medium heat, add the mushrooms and enough remaining water to achieve the desired consistency, and cook until the mushrooms are hot. Serve warm.

Veggie Pie

Yield: 8 servings

This hearty veggie pie surprised Brad into eating lots of brussels sprouts.

"This is much, much better than I expected. It makes brussels sprouts not suck so much." Would he eat it again? "Yes! But of course!" Would he eat it as leftovers? "Yes!" Would he ever make Veggie Pie for himself? "No! While I enjoyed it and would eat it again, I would not go through the effort of making it myself because it still has brussels sprouts in it."

The pie would also be a fabulous veggie pie without the brussels sprouts.

1 pound brussels sprouts, chopped
1 white potato, chopped
2 cups mixed frozen vegetables such as limas, chopped green
   beans, peas, and corn kernels
2 cups Mushroom Soup
1 cup vegan ground beef substitute
1 teaspoon Italian seasoning
1/2 teaspoon salt (optional)
1/4 teaspoon ground black pepper (optional)
1 (9-inch) Whole Wheat Pie Crust
   or 1 store-bought crust

Preheat the oven to 350 degrees F.

Place the brussels sprouts and the potato in a medium saucepan, with 1 cup water, and bring to a boil over high heat. Cover and reduce the heat to simmer 30 minutes or until the potato is tender and a knife can slide in easily; drain.

Place the frozen vegetables, soup, vegan ground beef substitute, and Italian seasoning in a large mixing bowl. Add salt and pepper, if using. Add the potato and brussels sprouts and stir until the ingredients are evenly distributed, but still chunky. Carefully pile the filling into the pie crust and smooth the mounded top. The filling should stick together and not spill over the edges. Bake 45 minutes.

Note: Instead of Mushroom Soup, extra vegetables may be used. Cook an additional half a potato with an additional 2 cups green vegetables (brussels sprouts, cabbage, celery or whatever is on hand). Put the extra veggies in a blender with the cooking water and puree until smooth.

Whole Wheat Pie Crust

Yield: one 8- or 9-inch pie crust

This crust for savory or sweet pies is almost as easy as picking one off the shelf and much more satisfying.

1 cup whole wheat pastry flour
1/4 teaspoon salt
1/4 cup vegetable oil
3 Tablespoons cold water

Preheat the oven to 375 degrees F.

Place the flour and salt in an 8- or 9-inch round pie pan and mix. Measure the oil in a liquid measuring cup; add the water. Beat the oil and water with a whisk or fork until emulsified. Pour the oil mixture over the flour and mix with a fork or your fingers until the dough is well blended. Press the dough evenly into the pan with your fingers and prick with a fork.

Bake for 7 minutes to firm the crust slightly before adding fillings. It will not be ready to eat yet. Follow a pie recipe for further baking instructions.

Note: For the best results, store the flour in the freezer and use ice-cold water.

Brad's Brussels Sprout Curry with Red Quinoa

Yield: 8 to 10 servings

Brad seemed competent in the kitchen. He knew what side of the knife cuts and how to stir. "It was less complicated than I anticipated it being. I don't generally cook. I consider anything more than three steps to be cooking. I assume that anything that I don't already know how to make is going to be complicated." Brad chopped and stirred while I assembled, washed, and measured. "Dinner was delicious! I would most assuredly look forward to eating it again. It was surprisingly yummy in spite of the brussels sprouts. I will not give them credit for anything. The rest of the ingredients really stepped up their game."

"So would you actually make it yourself?" I inquired with disbelief.

"Yes, I believe I would. It was easy."

1 large white potato, chopped
8 ounces brussels sprouts, chopped
1 small bunch bok choy, chopped
1 green bell pepper, chopped
1 cup red quinoa (or white quinoa)
2 Tablespoons olive oil
2 Tablespoons soy sauce
1 can (15 ounces) garbanzos, drained
1 cup canned water chestnuts, drained
1/2 bunch cilantro, 1/4 cup finely chopped cilantro (packed)
2 Tablespoons fresh ginger, finely chopped
2 teaspoons ground cumin
1/4 teaspoon salt (optional)
1 can (28 ounces) diced tomatoes, drained, 1/4 cup juice
  reserved
1 Tablespoon cornstarch

Put the vegetables in a large saucepan with 1 1/2 cups water and bring to a boil over high heat. Cover and reduce the heat to simmer for 30 minutes or until the potatoes are tender and a knife can slide in easily. Drain the cooking water. (It can be saved for vegetable stock.)

Place the quinoa in a fine-mesh strainer and rinse under running water. Place the quinoa and 2 cups water in a medium saucepan and bring to a boil over high heat. Cover and reduce the heat to simmer for 15 minutes or until the water is absorbed.

Meanwhile, place the oil and soy sauce in a large skillet over medium heat. Add the drained cooked vegetables and cook 5 minutes, stirring occasionally. Add the garbanzos, water chestnuts, cilantro, ginger, cumin, and salt, if using, to the vegetables and cook 2 minutes, stirring occasionally.

Mix the tomato juice with the cornstarch in a small bowl. Add the tomatoes and starchy tomato juice to the vegetables. Stir frequently as the sauce thickens. Remove from the heat when the sauce has thickened.

Mix the quinoa with the vegetables. Serve hot.

Note: If the listed green vegetables are not available, other vegetables such as cabbage, spinach, and celery may be substituted.

Brussels Sprout Quinoa Wraps: Leftovers make a great wrap filling for a lunch. Smear vegan mayonnaise and sprinkle nutritional yeast on a whole wheat tortilla. Fill with Brad's Brussels Sprout Curry with Red Quinoa. Serve warm or cold. The wrap can also be sliced and held with toothpicks for hors d'oeuvres.

Apple Mango Pie

Yield: 8 servings

I used brussels sprouts only because Brad dared me to find ways he would eat brussels sprouts. The beet provides reddish coloring to hide the green. Without either ingredient, the sauce will be a pleasant brown and the pie will taste just as good.

4 brussels sprouts (optional)
1/8 beet, chopped (optional)
10 pitted dates
1/4 cup maple syrup
2 Tablespoons vanilla soymilk
1 1/2 teaspoons cornstarch
1/2 teaspoon ground cinnamon
1/4 teaspoon salt (optional)
1/4 teaspoon vanilla extract
1/8 teaspoon ground nutmeg
3 apples, chopped in 1/2-inch pieces (about 3 cups, see note)
1 1/2 cups fresh chopped mango or slightly thawed frozen
  mango, chopped in 1/2-inch pieces
1 (9-inch) Whole Wheat Pie Crust or store-bought

Preheat the oven to 375 degrees F.

Put the brussels sprouts and beet, if using, in a small saucepan with 1/2 cup water and bring to a boil over high heat. Cover and reduce the heat to simmer for 20 minutes or until the beet is tender and a knife can slide in easily. Drain.

Place the brussels sprouts and beet in a blender. Add the dates, maple syrup, soymilk, cornstarch, cinnamon, salt (if using), vanilla, and nutmeg and process the mixture until it is smooth.

Place the apples and mango in a large mixing bowl. Pour the blended sauce over the fruit and stir. Put the filling into the pie crust. Bake for 45 minutes or until the apples are tender and a knife can slide in easily. Serve warm or cool with vegan ice cream.

Note: Use 3 different varieties of apples for a bounty of flavor.

Hickory Smoked Tofuphobic
Jeff Parimuha

Jeff Parimuha accepted a winter weekend invitation to my cabin in the snowbelt. "You're not going to feed me tofu are you?"

"There will be no tofu in the stew," I specifically promised, as I was planning tofu in the spinach dip and Jeff had agreed to try anything I prepared.

Jeff "Frombar" earned his name in my phone since I first met him at a bikers' bar. He asked my last name for his phone, which I spelled: D, i, n, s, h, a, h, a, h, a, h, a, h, a, q, u, e, s, n, y.

He said, "Wow, that's long! How do you pronounce it?"

"Let me see your phone." I read since I did not remember all the random letters after the extra ha ha, "Din-sha-ha-ha-ha-ha-ha-quesny." I explained the ancient Persian name, king of responsibilities and humor, as he pocketed his phone without suspicion.

Jeff was athletic enough to dig being with me. Shoveling our way into the driveway through layers of ice accumulated from passing snowplows, I marveled at his energy and handsomeness.

The cabin was as cold as the outdoors when we arrived. I had brought Spinach Artichoke Dip. Jeff scooped dip with tortilla chips. "Mmm. Yum," he commented. We fed each other so only one of our four hands was cold while we found ways to keep the other three hands warm. "The spinach dip was delightful. Unfortunately there wasn't very much of it," he teased after we ate our way through three cups of spinach dip and most of the bag of tortilla chips. "Spinach has good protein," he said.

"Spinach is better known for iron. I used soy for protein."

"I may not be able to tell you how much I like something, but you can tell by my actions."

"So by the empty dish I can surmise you like tofu?" I explained tofu is a form of soy.

"Tofu? Really? That was fantastic!"

Things were definitely heating up, including a Pumpkin Medley Pie, which we decided made a great second appetizer while we prepared dinner. We shared a fork and fed each other from the pan for fewer dishes to wash. Jeff had brought vegetables, wine, and candles. We created Jeff Eight Veggie Stew, which we enjoyed with baked potatoes. "Hey! This is good!" he declared, amazed at his vegetable preparing proficiency.

Jeff's brother called from a deer-hunting trip. When Jeff told him he was at my cabin, his brother responded, "A vegan? What the hell are you doing?"

"I like vegetables. It'll be all right. I'm interested to see how it will go." Jeff said.

At age fourteen Jeff was a pedestrian hit by a car and hospitalized for four weeks. He craved all vegetables and has liked them ever since. He grew two inches and amazed the doctors with a full recovery from severe head trauma, broken nose, cracked orbital bone, whiplash, broken arm, and assorted abrasions and contusions.

Jeff is an awesome guy, a spirited conversationalist, energetic, good in the kitchen, and optimistic. "As I grow older and as of yet am childless, I have found that the best way for my legacy to live on is through the memories of others. With all the negativity existing in the world I attempt to impart a positive influence on those lives in which I interact." He attributes a lot of his personal philosophy to the research he did and discipline he learned while attaining his black belt in tae kwon do.

The next day Jeff quoted Red Green as he fixed my broken snow shovel, "If the women don't find you handsome, they should at least find you handy." He did dishes out at the well in a blizzard, then I let him search for places to warm his hands. I handed him a bowl of hot Revamped Veggie Stew. We baked Chococheesecake together after he leveled my old tailgate countertop. Jeff summarized his meals. "I didn't really know what to expect eating vegan.

I like to try new things. My taste buds and palate were immensely satisfied."

Under the hickory trees we confirmed that I can kiss a meat-eater, but I cannot kiss a smoker. (Jeff's photo page 18)

Spinach Artichoke Dip

Yield: 3 cups

This creamy dip packs subtle flavors. Tofu skeptics will love it.

1 small yellow onion, finely diced
1 small bunch spinach, chopped
1 Tablespoon olive oil
1 Tablespoon soy sauce
1 teaspoon rosemary
1/2 teaspoon caraway seeds
5 ounces firm tofu, rinsed, drained, and crumbled
1/2 cup plain soymilk
1/4 cup vegan mayonnaise
1 teaspoon lemon juice
1 cup canned artichoke hearts (not marinated), drained
  and chopped

Place the oil in a small skillet over medium-high heat. Add the onion and soy sauce to the pan. Cook, stirring occasionally, for 5 to 7 minutes or until the onion is translucent and the edges are browned. Add the spinach, cover the pan, and cook 2 additional minutes to wilt the spinach.

Put the rosemary and caraway seeds in a blender with a tight lid. Process until the seasonings become a combination of particles and half-sized pieces. Add the tofu, soymilk, mayonnaise, and lemon juice to the blender. Process until the mixture is smooth.

Put the tofu mixture in a small bowl. Add the onions, spinach, and artichoke to the tofu mixture and mix thoroughly.

Refrigerate 1 hour to thicken. Serve with chips, veggies, or pita.

Pumpkin Medley Pie

Yield: 16 servings (2 pies)

Not a typical pumpkin pie, this one contains chunks of pleasure. Jeff said, "The pineapple and pumpkin complement each other well. The hint of walnuts is perfect in this setting for a winter season flavor." Two pies are better than one!

3 medium yams or large sweet potatoes, peeled and chopped
1 can (29 ounces) pumpkin
3/4 cup raw cane sugar crystals
1/2 cup maple syrup
1 Tablespoon pumpkin pie spices
1 Tablespoon cornstarch
1/2 teaspoon salt (optional)
1 can (14 ounces) pineapple tidbits, drained (about 2 cups)
3/4 cup walnuts, chopped
2 (9-inch) Whole Wheat Pie Crusts (p. 69) or 2 store-bought
   crusts

Preheat the oven to 350 degrees F. Place the yams in a medium saucepan, add 1 cup water, and bring to a boil over high heat. Cover and reduce the heat to simmer for 30 minutes or until the yams are tender and a knife can slide in easily. Drain.

Place the pumpkin, sugar, maple syrup, spices, cornstarch, and salt, if using, in a large bowl and mix. Add the yams, drained pineapple, and walnuts to the pumpkin mixture and mix gently until completely blended but still chunky. Divide the filling into the two crusts and smooth the tops with a spatula. Bake for 40 minutes or until the tops of the pies begin to brown.

Jeff Eight Veggie Stew

Yield: 8 servings

Jeff's three favorite vegetables are "the green ones, the orange ones, and the yellow ones." We opted to make a vegetable stew that would heat us from the inside out on a cold December day. I had Chinese cabbage, carrots, and bok choy. Jeff asked what he could bring and received instructions to bring at least three more vegetables of varying colors. Stew tastes great with baked potatoes.

1 large carrot, chopped
3 bell peppers, chopped (red, orange, yellow, or one of each)
1 small head broccoli, chopped
1 small bunch bok choy, chopped
1/4 head Chinese cabbage, chopped
5 Brussels sprouts, chopped
8 ounces green beans, chopped
8 ounces portobello mushrooms, chopped
4 cups water
1/2 bunch fresh parsley, 1/4 cup chopped packed (optional)
1/4 teaspoon ground cayenne pepper (optional)
1/4 teaspoon ground celery seed (optional)
1/4 teaspoon ground paprika (optional)
1/4 teaspoon salt (optional)

Place all the vegetables and the water in a large saucepan and bring to a boil over high heat. Cover, reduce the heat to simmer 20 minutes or until the carrot is tender and a knife can slide in easily. Add the seasonings, if using, and serve.

Revamped Veggie Stew: "This smells great! What is it? When did you make this?" Jeff asked as new stew magically appeared in seconds the next day. To enhance vegetable stew leftovers, reheat with tomato sauce, beans (canned, drained), and black olives (canned, drained). This stew is often more popular than the original and rarely recognized. Jeff said, "The stew has so many flavors it is just as good as any animal stew. It tastes complete without the meat!"

Chococheesecake

Yield: 8 servings

"I thought it WAS cheesecake. I really liked it. Then I remembered helping make it with tofu. I swallowed my tofu-disparaging pride and asked for another piece," said Jeff.

Graham Cracker Crust
7 graham crackers, crumbled (1 1/4 cups)
3 Tablespoons oil
1 Tablespoon water

Cheesecake
1 pound soft tofu, rinsed, drained, and crumbled
1 cup maple syrup
1/2 cup unsweetened cocoa powder
3 Tablespoons lemon juice
3 Tablespoons vegan margarine
1 teaspoon vanilla extract
1 teaspoon cornstarch
1/2 teaspoon salt
1 cup raspberries, sliced nectarines, or other fresh fruit

Preheat the oven to 350 degrees F.

For the graham cracker crust: Mix the graham cracker crumbs with the oil and water in a 9-inch round baking dish and press it to the bottom. Bake the crust for 7 minutes.

For the cheesecake: Put the tofu, maple syrup, cocoa powder, lemon juice, margarine, vanilla, cornstarch, and salt in a blender. Process until the mixture is smooth. Pour the filling into the crust. Bake 45 minutes.

Allow the cheesecake to cool to room temperature to set, then refrigerate for at least 1 hour. Top with the raspberries and serve.

Note: Store bought crust may be used. However, try to get one without hydrogenated oils, certainly without lard for a vegan.

Addicted to Death

Robert Crane

I fell for Robert Crane on our first date. I was new to town and he responded to my Internet personal ad for a Columbus tour guide. We met at a coffee shop, although I don't drink coffee nor do I like to shop. He glided in, looking dashing in his long black trench coat. I tried to ignore the unmistakable leather cloaking his tall, sturdy frame as we decided to tour downtown on foot. Leaving the coffee shop, my gaze was still upon him. I did not notice the steps, fell hard on my knees, and bounced right back up quickly.

Robert is intelligent, articulate, strong, and likes clothes shopping. His true love is theater; he enjoys playing dress-up. On our second date I let him examine my closet to pick my attire for going dancing together. I wound up wearing a lacy little black shirt from his closet! For our third date we went shopping together because my wardrobe was "much more conducive to living in a cabin than dating in Columbus, or anywhere for that matter," he said. We toured the second-hand stores where he set right to work examining the overwhelming possibilities as if it were a theatrical costume warehouse. And who better to tell me what a man would like to see me wear than a man?

Robert admits he is a food hypocrite. Perhaps the challenge of his idiosyncrasies is part of my attraction to him. Robert hates onions and greasy foods, but likes onion rings. He likes peanuts and cashews, but no other nuts, and they cannot be an ingredient in anything, just eaten out of hand. He likes fruit juice, fruit jells, and fruit, but will not eat a fruit jell with chunks of fruit in it. He will only eat foods of the same texture in each bite. He does not like blueberries or muffins, but blueberry muffins are the only kind of muffin he will eat. He likes fig newtons, but refuses to try eating a fig. His favorite color is purple, but he will not eat eggplant, plums, or anything else purple except black grapes.

Robert likes meat, but will not eat vegan meat substitutes. "It's missing something," he told me once.

Although I am usually one to tread lightly around differences, I felt comfortable enough with Robert to say what I was really thinking, "Missing what? Like death?"

"Exactly. Death. Fear. Blood. You can't fake that." His complete matter-of-fact agreement surprised me. I decided to save further discussion on the topic for another time.

We made Robert's Dinner, an oversized dollop of thick mashed potatoes on a plate, smashed down in the center to form a bowl, filled with pasta, and slathered it all in pasta sauce. We made this meal a few times for each other, sometimes with a side salad and/or bread. It works with instant mashed potatoes and a jar of sauce, but tastes better from real potatoes and fresh vegetables in the sauce.

"It's yummy starch upon yummy carbs and starch with a nice colorful marinara-based sauce to add some sweetness and veggie food groups to the mix," he declared.

Late one Sunday evening Robert craved Chinese food and I was up for it. He asked whether I would be offended if he ate meat in front of me, if there are things I can eat at a Chinese restaurant, and where else I would consider going if we arrived as they were closing for the night. He respected my values and had genuine concern for my food happiness. I assured him I would find a vegetable dish, but he didn't seem to relax until I was actually eating. The most memorable part of the evening was that, according to Robert, when one reads a fortune cookie, there is an implied "in bed" at the end of the saying.

Our fortunes that evening:

Anne: "If you develop the habits of success, you will make success a habit."

Robert: "An hour with a friend is better than ten with a stranger."

Robert's meals with me required no recipes.

A Model Date for a Vegan

Oliver Claypool

Oliver Claypool was the master of disguise, his thin frame draped in a white-with-stripes button-down business shirt, looking too geeky for a Friday evening date as he met me at the restaurant door. He was just another one in a long series of first dates, none of whom inspired me to write anything substantial or go on a second date. I held no expectations for him other than to consume a meal and a couple hours. I humbly admitted later that a computer showed better judgment picking Oliver for me.

We were impressed with neither the menu nor the lamb special of the day option. As I studied the yellowing map of Turkey against the magenta wall, Oliver apologized for picking the restaurant and offered to take me elsewhere. I did not tell him my vegan secret, yet he agreed to share the vegetarian sampler platter. His amiable nature gained him the first ounce of my interest.

Oliver seemed intelligent and pleasant enough to continue the evening beyond dinner. He asked if I wanted to accompany him to a games night at his friend's house. "I want to invite you, but..." his pause indicated there was going to be a unique situation, "my friends are nudists. We don't have to take our clothes off. It's just board games, no Twister or anything."

I decided to be cautiously adventurous and brought my own car; if I felt trapped in an awkward situation I could leave gracefully. Oliver divulged that the nudist conversation was a test of my suitability for meeting his friends open-mindedly; they would be clothed. His friends tipped me off that Oliver was writing a book about dating. He mentioned wanting to see me again. I asked, "Does that mean you are interested in a second date or mere fodder for your book?"

"I don't write about everyone in my book," he said. "Just the dates who are either crazy-different or the ones I really like."

"Which am I?" I inquired, only to be met with a smirk. "Or which would you like me to be?" He had no inkling I hoped to write about him too.

The morning preceding our second date, I nervously requested our third date, an Italian feast meetup group requiring an RSVP. His texted reply was perfect, "A beautiful woman and Italian food. Sounds great!"

We had been assigned to make ciamotta, a laborious recipe of overly fried potatoes, eggplant, and peppers. He wore a soft gray t-shirt that hinted of a sculpted body enclosing the personality with which I had become infatuated. We talked about the menu items others would bring, including noodles with rabbit sauce. My companion rabbits would appreciate it if he made a good choice. He deduced my veggie ways and asked me what would happen if he ate meat in my presence. I responded, "I'm sure you have eaten meat prior to this meal. I also know you own a toothbrush. You will have to make your own decision."

Oliver declined the main dish of lamb, despite the persistence of the proud host. Oliver explained that although he is not vegetarian, he is "vegetarian sympathetic." He declined the rabbit noodles in favor of twenty meatless dishes. During the third hour of the feast, he whispered that his fridge is usually vegetarian; my heart melted to his words—and to his gentle touch near the hem of my skirt under the table. Each new thing I learned about him made me like him more.

Oliver works as an investment accountant; his nerd shirt on our first date cleverly disguised an alluring model's body. He loves to eat healthy and only occasionally eats meat, socially or when trying a specific new recipe. More than a muse for my writing and inspiration for the following recipes, I found a companion for a potential serious relationship. Oliver became the perfect last date for *Dating Vegans* as we planned to be the final chapter, the success story for each other's dating books.

Cinnamon Rolls

Yield: 16 rolls

These are easier to make than the recipe might look. They require a little advance planning, but are well worth the wait. A whiff of these rolls baking will draw people to the kitchen to help eat them.

2 cups vanilla soymilk
1/2 cup vegetable oil
3/4 cup raw cane sugar crystals
1 Tablespoon active dry baking yeast
3 1/4 cups whole wheat pastry flour
1 1/2 cups unbleached all-purpose flour
1 1/2 teaspoons baking powder
1 teaspoon salt
3 Tablespoons vegan margarine
2 teaspoons ground cinnamon
1 cup pecans, finely chopped
1/2 cup maple syrup

Place the soymilk, oil, and 1/2 cup of the sugar in a large saucepan and whisk to blend. Heat over medium-high until the mixture just begins to boil; watch closely to be sure it doesn't boil over. Remove the saucepan from the heat and allow the mixture to cool to lukewarm, about 45 minutes.

Add the baking yeast to the liquid. Allow the liquid to sit for 1 minute and the yeast to bubble. Mix 3 cups of the pastry flour and 1 cup of the all-purpose flour into the liquid. Cover the dough and let sit for 1 hour in a warm place.

Place the remaining 1/2 cup all-purpose flour, baking powder, and salt in a bowl and mix to combine, then stir into the dough.

Sprinkle some of the remaining 1/4 cup pastry flour on a large cutting board or counter. Place the dough on the flour. Sprinkle some of the flour on the dough. Roll out the dough to form a rough 12 x 15-inch rectangle.

Place the margarine in a small saucepan and melt over medium-low heat. Drizzle the melted margarine on the dough and spread it evenly. Sprinkle the remaining 1/4 cup sugar and cinnamon on the margarine.

Carefully roll the dough into a log, towards you, lengthwise from the farthest edge. If it looks like the margarine might run off the dough on the near end, lift the last couple inches of the dough onto the log instead of bringing the log onto the edge. Pinch the seam with wet fingers.

Preheat the oven to 400 degrees F. Lightly oil a large baking sheet.

Slice the dough log into 3/4- to 1-inch slices. Carefully pick up each slice and place it on its side in the pan, cut side up, leaving an inch between each roll. Let the rolls sit in a warm place for 30 minutes, until they have risen and are touching each other. Bake the rolls for 10 to 12 minutes or until they begin to look golden, but remain a hint moist on the top.

Mix the pecans with the maple syrup. Spoon the pecan maple mixture onto the top center area of each roll; spilling onto other areas of the rolls is acceptable. Bake an additional 5 minutes or until the rolls are golden and the nuts begin to toast.

Serve the rolls warm. The rolls should easily separate from each other.

Hidden Treasure Peppers

Yield: 6 servings

Do not be fooled by the light and flaky exterior of this casserole. Its hearty filling will satisfy any meat-and-potatoes eater.

4 white potatoes, chopped
1/2 cup plain soymilk
1 yellow, green, or red bell pepper, chopped
2 Tablespoons chopped fresh basil, or 1 Tablespoon dried basil

A Model Date for a Vegan

1 cup vegan sausage meat substitute
1/4 cup nutritional yeast
1 Tablespoon soy sauce
1 teaspoon sesame seeds (optional)
1/4 teaspoon ground black pepper (optional)
1/4 teaspoon salt (optional)
1/4 cup olive oil
8 sheets phyllo dough (12-inch squares)

Place the potatoes in a medium-sized saucepan, add 2 cups water, and bring to a boil over high heat. Cover and reduce the heat to simmer for 30 minutes or until the potatoes are tender and a knife can slide in easily. Drain and mash the potatoes. Add the soy-milk and mix.

Add the bell pepper, basil, sausage, yeast, soy sauce to the potatoes. If using optional ingredients: sesame seeds, black pepper, and salt, add to the potatoes. Mix.

Preheat the oven to 375 degrees F. Lightly oil the bottom and sides of an 8-inch square casserole pan. Place one sheet of phyllo dough in the bottom of the pan. Let the excess dough hang over the sides of the pan. Use a pastry brush to brush the phyllo lightly with the oil. Place the second sheet of phyllo on top of the first and brush with the oil. Repeat the process for a total of 4 phyllo sheet layers.

Place the potato filling in the pan on the phyllo. Lightly pack down the filling so the top is flat. Layer 3 of the remaining sheets of the phyllo dough on top, brushing each one with the oil before putting the next one over it. Fold the edges of the phyllo dough over the casserole and tuck in the sides. Add the top layer of the phyllo neatly to cover the casserole and brush the very top lightly with the oil. Bake for 30 minutes, or until the phyllo top begins to turn brown and flaky.

Note: If the phyllo sheets are not perfect, pieces can be hidden in the layers. Try to keep one nice phyllo sheet for the top layer.

Oliver's Spinach Strata

Yield: 8 servings

This lasagna-like casserole is not called lasagna because lasagna implies a pre-conceived cheese taste. Oliver said, "This is deliciously different, equally tasty." It is easy to assemble because the noodles are not boiled in advance—they are placed in the casserole dry, and the liquid from the other ingredients softens them as the casserole bakes. The baking time creates a leisurely hour for other activities.

3 cans (15 ounces each) great northern beans, drained
  (about 4 1/2 cups)
2 Tablespoons nutritional yeast
1 Tablespoon olive oil
2 teaspoons Italian seasoning
1 teaspoon turmeric
1 large can (28 ounces) tomato sauce (about 3 cups)
8 ounces (1 small bunch) fresh spinach, or thawed frozen
8 sheets whole wheat lasagna
8 ounces white button or portobello mushrooms, chopped

Preheat the oven to 350 degrees F. Lightly oil a 9 x 13-inch casserole pan.

Pour the beans into a large bowl and mash them with masher or fork. Add the yeast, oil, Italian seasonings, and turmeric to the beans and mix. Set the bean mixture aside.

Wash the spinach in warm water to help it begin to wilt. Drain all the water from the spinach and chop it. Cover the bottom of the pan with 1/2 cup of the tomato sauce and half of the spinach. Put 4 pieces of pasta on the spinach. Spread 1/2 cup more tomato sauce on the pasta.

Spread half of the mushrooms on the sauce. Add the remaining spinach and pack down lightly.

Gently spread half of the bean mixture evenly over the spinach, which will help condense the spinach. Put the remaining 4 pieces of pasta on the beans. Spread the remaining mushrooms and beans on top of the pasta. Top with the remaining 2 cups of sauce, spreading evenly to completely cover the beans, mushrooms and pasta. Bake uncovered for 1 hour or until pasta is tender to a fork.

Note: The pan should be full but not overflow as the sauce cooks. The spinach will condense as it cooks. If the pan is so full that the sauce might bubble over, place a baking sheet under the pan.

Peach-Oatmeal Muffins

Yield: 12 large muffins

This recipe originally appeared in *Healthy Hearty Helpings* as Peach-Oatmeal Breakfast Muffins. They are also a great snack or simple meal any time of the day. The long list of ingredients may look daunting, but they are as easy to make as they are to eat.

3 peaches, chopped
1 cup strawberries, hulled and chopped (optional)
3 bananas, mashed
1 cup raspberry juice or other fruit juice
3/4 cup applesauce
1/2 cup maple syrup
3 cups whole wheat pastry flour or unbleached flour
1 cup quick oats
1 Tablespoon cornstarch
1 teaspoon baking soda
1 teaspoon ground cinnamon
1/4 teaspoon salt (optional)
3/4 cup chopped pitted dates
1/2 cup chopped walnuts or other nuts

Preheat the oven to 375 degrees F. Lightly oil a large muffin tin (or use a nonstick tin).

Place the peaches, strawberries (if using), bananas, juice, applesauce, and maple syrup in a large bowl and mix. Place the flour, oats, cornstarch, baking soda, cinnamon, and salt, if using, in a separate bowl and mix. Combine the mixtures and mix again. Add the dates and walnuts to the muffin batter and mix. Place the batter in the prepared muffin tin. Bake for 30 minutes or until light brown and dry on top except for the melted fruit.

Note: You can easily substitute other types of fruit such as apples, pears, or blueberries in this recipe. If your date hates chunks of nuts, you can grind the nuts instead of chopping them, or omit them. (Using ground nuts may slightly reduce the flour necessary.) Experiment with other spices such as ginger. Old-fashioned oats make the muffins heartier than quick oats.

Chocolate Macadamia Nut Cookies

Yield: 44 small cookies or 32 medium cookies

"Absolutely scrumptious!" said Oliver.

> 4 ounces unsweetened baker's chocolate
> 1/4 cup vegan margarine
> 2 cups whole wheat pastry flour
> 1 1/4 cups raw cane sugar crystals
> 1/2 teaspoon baking powder
> 1/4 teaspoon salt (not needed if using salted nuts)
> 1 banana, mashed
> 1/2 cup maple syrup
> 1/3 cup vanilla soymilk
> 1 teaspoon vanilla extract
> 1 1/2 cup roasted macadamia nuts
> 1/2 cup semisweet chocolate chunks

Preheat the oven to 350 degrees F. Line two baking sheets with parchment paper.

Place the chocolate and margarine in a double boiler and melt them over medium high heat. Meanwhile, put the flour, sugar, baking powder and salt in a large bowl and mix. Add the banana to the dry ingredients.

When the chocolate mixture has melted, remove it from the heat. Add the maple syrup, soymilk, and vanilla to the chocolate and mix. Add the chocolate mixture to the dry ingredients and mix. The dough should be a stiff peanut butter consistency.

Add the nuts and chocolate chunks to the dough. Mix enough to distribute the chunks throughout the dough. Drop the cookie dough by heaping tablespoons onto the parchment. Leave at least an inch between cookies for expansion. Keep most of the nuts tucked into the chocolate dough.

Bake for 15 to 18 minutes, or until the cookies are soft and moist, but not wet, and any protruding nuts are roasted to a golden brown. The cookies will harden as they cool. Serve warm or cool.

Note: Store the cookies in the refrigerator. The cookies may also be frozen for later use, although they are just as good to eat straight from the freezer so do not plan on freezing to extend their existence.

Double Chocolate Cookies

Oliver said he doesn't like nuts in his desserts so I made two batches of the above recipe. For the second batch, I substituted an additional cup of chocolate chunks for the macadamia nuts, which resulted in two great cookie recipes! However, I baked the nutty ones before he arrived for dinner. When I turned to check the oven on his double chocolate cookies, one of the nutty ones disappeared from the plate. I laughed as he tried to pretend he wasn't up to anything. He decided he likes nuts in these cookies and admitted both flavors are irresistible.

Reflections on Dating Nonvegans

Compatibility and Chemistry

Compatibility can be established gradually. Relationship, lifestyle, and values questions can be answered over time. People can choose what to compromise, learn what is naturally compatible, and discover what is a deal-breaker. See vegan compatibility issues (p. 110).

Chemistry is much more difficult to predict and quantify. Each person must weigh how much chemistry and compatibility are necessary in a relationship. The couples' stories (p. 134) help solve the mysteries of relationships between a vegan and a nonvegan.

Terrific men, both romantic dates and friends, inspired a myriad of recipes while sharing marvelous experiences. I rekindled a love of cooking and writing. But did I really think God would let me get away with writing about dating without falling in love with a man?

Oliver surprised me in becoming a wonderful tale. From the first date I knew he would at least be worthy of a short story. We seemed compatible and it was easy to dream of a long-term relationship that he was gently seeking. He asked about my previous relationships in regards to their vegan status. I usually date men who are not vegan to which he openly concluded that I am converting the world to vegan one man at a time. I teased him not to become vegan too quickly as it could end our relationship.

After an evening out with friends, I invited him to remove his black wool coat and stay a while. Partly I wanted to spend time together, partly because cuddling a wool coat is disgustingly itchy. But I knew something was not right. He confirmed my suspicions; he didn't want to waste my time pursuing a long-term relationship. He wasn't feeling the chemistry.

I know now why I did not cry. Oliver hadn't hurt me. He was just his honest, good-natured nice-guy self. We shared an experience. Life is unscripted, especially between writers and/or daters.

Reflections on Dating Nonvegans

The saying goes that it is better to have loved and lost, than never to have loved at all. I did not love and lose. I loved and learned.

I had the answer to the question from the Dave story (p. 59). Could I love a man who ate meat? And owned a freezer full of it? I thought about Jennie's deal with her husband Dan (p. 158). Dan has one drawer in the fridge for meat and one designated "pan of death." Perhaps I could not tolerate a whole freezer, maybe just a drawer in the fridge.

I accepted Oliver's lack of chemistry without argument over that which I cannot control. Now I pretended to bargain with the devil, but I knew it was just unrequited love throwing me a fictitious answer for a vegan dating book.

I have always believed the best gift anyone can give is time spent together. I would not alter any part of Oliver's terrific personality, and choose to accept him as the person he is. Oliver and I would grow to be great friends as he suggested. As I wrote, the words flowed, and so finally did the tears.

I read this passage to Oliver the evening I wrote it. I needed closure to our romantic dating to be free to try the new role as great friends. He gave me his attention while baking me his first vegan pumpkin pie. Oliver's pumpkin pie recipe cannot be contained in this book or any other publication. Although he shared the recipe with me and gave his permission to use it, I immediately forgot on purpose because it is the intangible ingredients that made it incredible. The pie could never be re-created to the excellence he did that evening, full of passion and fervor. The graham crust, burned from my reading distraction, held the smoothest tawny delight. Every morsel tasted perfect.

Confluence

Ingredients: The single men contained in this book...

    Fed me...the creativity for recipes

    Touched me...with their honesty

    Held me...to a high standard

    Trusted me...to unveil them

    Loved me...for myself

    Encouraged me...to continue to date nonvegan men

Confluence means a coming together. I decided I like the word confluence better than conclusion, because this is not the end of my dating, but a coming together of my thoughts. Confluence Park, where the Olentangy and Scioto Rivers meet in downtown Columbus, seemed the perfect destination for a bicycle journey as my thoughts rolled along.

I thought about Robert and Oliver, my two friends with whom I spent the most time recently. Both began in the romantic date category although they are very different. My thoughts sifted back through everyone whose stories emerged on these pages....all the way back to Paul. Paul and I thought we were only having dinner and testing to see if I could write anything useful about eating vegan food together.

We didn't dream it would become *Dating Vegans*.

Packaging: Robert reminds me I am alluring; beauty on the outside deserves to be flaunted. I need to see in myself what he sees in me. One particular shopping excursion Robert compiled a varied stack of clothes for me to try. Robert noticed I neglected an item... the leather halter top. I told him it was leather and I was not going to get it so there was no point in trying. His dejected look convinced me to put it on for a few seconds. The multitude of metal fasteners confused me and I required his assistance in adjusting. Then he turned me toward the mirror where I did not recognize the slutty vixen staring back at me. She had power! He said, "You should get in touch with your inner dominatrix."

For a moment, I was tempted. The top was certainly different from anything I owned and surprisingly it did not smell like raunchy old leather. Despite being at a second-hand store it was new, unworn, with the original tags, and significantly marked down. It could be mine for only twelve dollars, and well worth it. I would receive twelve dollars' worth of drinks from suitors in the first public minute of wearing this thing, if I had the courage to wear it... or if I drank.

But it had been worn before. As I refused to purchase the top, my mind played a video of a cow, hanging upside-down from her hoof, writhing in pain with her throat slit, blood pumping out, terrified in her last living moments. She had worn it before me, proudly, where it belonged. I could not take her hand-me-down clothing since it was not given willingly. Robert was disappointed with my decision, but he expected it. He pointed out that my skin would only touch the satin interior; the leather was on the outside. He did not win this discussion.

Robert reminded me I am beautiful to him. "Your clothes are about bringing the outer packaging up to match the great qualities on the inside."

I thought a lot about the top recently. It does not matter how many dates it might have gotten me. If I am not true to myself, who am I? For one moment I liked the leather-clad woman in the mirror: her look conveyed adventure, confidence, and beauty. However, the compassionate woman who possesses those qualities quickly made the vegan choice. I always try to make the best decisions possible with all the information I have. I confidently concluded I could never parade around in someone else's skin and then expect a man to take me seriously in my own.

Contents: I thought about my amazing bookends, the first and last stories of my dating section, Paul and Oliver. I consider them to be two of my rarest friends, people who I allow to influence me at times because they have earned my trust. They both are very honest and certain I am not who they want to romantically date, but place higher value in our friendships.

Once for a class assignment I had to ask people to describe me in five words. Paul came up with: caring, adventurous, hard-working, competitive, and friendly. For fun conversation on a long road trip Oliver and I described each other, but the fifth word had to have a negative connotation. He said I am caring, adventurous, down-to-earth, an animal-lover, and ridiculous. (Yes, he really did list the exact same two qualities first!) The qualities that Paul and Oliver notice define me, not "hot in leather."

Although Oliver is a model, he is refreshingly unconcerned about clothes. Oliver pretends not to notice my outer packaging, but I know he must. He reminds me about my terrific qualities on the inside, my unmistakable genuine personality and quality of character. Oliver accepts my veganism as inherent ethics tied to strong emotions. He does not test the strength of my convictions. We value each other's opinions. We contribute ideas for each other's dating books as we share our journeys and seek our goals. I value his friendship, honesty, and companionship; his contents… and his packaging.

Paul has seen me at what I consider my least attractive: ex-hausted, dirty, drenched in sweat, hair in a huge tangled mess, and sometimes frustrated with myself as he taught me to wrestle. Paul is incredibly charismatic, logical, and thoughtful; qualities I have been fortunate to discover under his handsome exterior with a stoic facade. He said people rarely take the time to get to know him as I have. He told me once that it is easy for him to see how people are attracted to me; he finds my wit, charm, humor, and wordplay endearing. Although he acknowledges that some men may be attracted to me physically, it is the beautiful person he sees inside who makes me his very good friend. Paul likes that I am ambitious, interesting, helpful, and optimistic. He suggested that some of these qualities are why I can date meat-eaters.

Reflections on Dating Nonvegans

My bookends give me hope that there are more terrific guys out there. Paul and Oliver are strong, intelligent, compassionate men who inspire me with their humorous positive attitudes and witty comments. I remembered writing something last year, a list of qualities I find desirable in men; not that I expected to find all these, just more of a guide of what I personally look for before vegan. I wanted to gain perspective on why I am able to date men who are not vegan. I found the list and noticed that for Paul and Oliver I easily check off all the first fifteen qualities I like in men. The sixteenth box is vegan (p. 14).

Someday there will be a man to share my life with every day until I am over one hundred years old. Perhaps he will be initially lured by my physical qualities, but more importantly he will appreciate my core values. He will respect me for being genuine, honest, enthusiastic, and whatever else is contained in his top fifteen ideal qualities of a woman. He will fall in love with a vegan.

How to Get From the First Date to Forever

Recipes for Long-term Relationships

Getting from the first date to forever, a couple must go beyond the one meal outings. Share a whole day (three or more meals!) take a trip together, spend the night, and discover if you are really as into each other as you dreamed you might be. Do a few hours inspire you to contemplate a lifetime together?

Dating Vegans

Long-Distance Dating and the Multi-day Date

Long-distance dating requires the use of phone, email, or other communication each of which is missing the component of physical contact. When two people in a long-distance relationship finally do get together, instead of one date for a few hours, they have the pressure of the multi-day date. Results may be similar to when two people in a new relationship progress beyond the one-meal outings. Allow me to share a story:

Rodney is intelligent, athletic, and healthy. With a happy dose of humor thrown into his well-sculpted six-foot, four-inch frame, he is a joy to hang out with, a deep thinker who finds the fun in life. We met at an animal rights gathering where we immediately felt a connection beyond compassion for animals. Unfortunately he lives in Canada.

He sings in a band that plays a fusion of music. He writes words and melodies and helps with arrangement of the band's original songs. When hanging with the band he consumes primarily pizza, burgers, chips, and beer. At home he eats mostly fresh food from his garden: tomatoes, spinach, beets, peppers, Swiss chard, cabbage, rutabaga, raspberries, lettuce, chives, onions, garlic, mint, parsley, and basil.

I had not sampled his cooking prior to my visit, but there was enough chemistry between Rodney and me that I drove 4 1/2 hours to see him. I arrived ready for catch-up cuddle 'n' conversation. I was so happy to be with him, eating seemed optional. When dinnertime quickly approached, I giggled at his hairnet and culinary enthusiasm.

We shared a terrific salad from his garden, a fresh and tasty mix of lettuces, spinach, and purple beans with beautiful nasturtium flowers packing a healthy radish-like bite of color. The dressing added a light accent from the combination of leftover juice from the bottom of a sweet pickle jar combined with a splash of olive oil, balsamic vinegar, and basil (all amounts to taste).

Good thing I kissed the cook prior to eating his garlic mashed potatoes. I appreciated my host's efforts and agreed to eat as many raw onion pieces as he did. I forgot to mention garlic and onion are my least favorite vegetables. I never got garlic breath because it could not fight its way past my serious onion breath. We joked about him sabotaging my dating recipes and decided not to recommend his potatoes. Instead of dessert, we swished mouthwash.

People date because they like to spend time together. Time together exhibits personal qualities that are endearing or annoying which bring people together or drive them further apart. Long-distance dating is automatically contrary to time together, especially when neither person wants to live where the other one lives.

Rodney and I realized we were not as compatible as needed for being serious, despite a strong chemistry. Therefore we put no pressure or hopes on each other except to enjoy the days we spent together and not pursue our romantic connection. I believe there is a saying, "Think Globally, Date Locally." It saves gas and heartache.

Another complication in long-distance dating is that one is committed to spending the night, which may mean various things. For us it meant I got to wake up in Rodney's large, strong, comfortable arms. Even better was Rodney's Berry Best Oatmeal. So full of flavor it did not need any brown sugar, soymilk, or other things routinely added to oatmeal. The best oatmeal I have ever eaten! Definitely worth sleeping-over.

For people in a long-distance relationship with someone who might be "the right one" I wish you happiness, hope, and the fortitude to persist. Long distances can provide a great opportunity for exploring each other's minds. I am living proof that a long-distance relationship works for some people: My parents started as pen pals.

Rodney's Berry Best Oatmeal

Yield: 2 hearty servings

This hot breakfast is worth waking up for any time of the year!

2 1/2 cups water
3 1/2 cups mulberries, raspberries, and strawberries
  or other fresh berries
3/4 cup granola
2/3 cup quick oats

Put the water in a medium saucepan and bring to a boil over high heat. Add the remaining ingredients and stir. Remove the saucepan from the heat, cover, and let sit until the oatmeal thickens. Serve the oatmeal in a large bowl to share with someone special as breakfast in bed. Remember the spoons and napkins.

Note: If using frozen berries instead of fresh, put the berries in the water prior to bringing water to a boil.

Perhaps Philip (p. 54) is gathering berries to try this recipe?

Breakfast

Breakfast is the most important meal of the day. And in dating it can be the most awkward. It is good for the nonvegan person to have on hand a few things such as a vegan whole grain healthy cereal, soymilk, fresh fruit, bagels, and vegan margarine just in case that first breakfast together happens before there is a chance to whip up a batch of the more time-consuming Cinnamon Rolls.

Rodney's Berry Best Oatmeal exhibits oatmeal as a taste sensation. However, having a simple box of quick oats and some water can suffice to create oatmeal and stave away hunger if needed. A little maple syrup, brown sugar, cinnamon, or sliced banana on top helps too.

Time-honored toast (from vegan bread) is good with vegan margarine, fruit preserves, or beans (very popular in England). Vegan frozen waffles are becoming readily available as is nondairy yogurt. Any form of fried potatoes or applesauce is popular with many people. Fruit salad can be delightful. Smoothies can easily be concocted in the blender with soymilk, frozen fruit, and a banana.

Nick's Classic Pancakes are ideal when a leisurely breakfast is desired. Flipping pancakes provides the opportunity to create fun in the kitchen together.

Some dates might just love another helping of dessert from the night before or even the main course. Meanwhile, Peach-Oatmeal Muffins are great to have available if the date has to run out the door quickly …to go to work, of course.

Holidays and Other Occasions

Christmas

One never knows when the opportunity will arise to share the spirit of Christmas. Last year the day after Christmas was my Christmas. I spent the day with Hank, helping him sift through piles of charcoal debris that had been his home. Many people had offered to help him clean it more quickly, but I was one of the few he trusted to sort through his home with the care it takes to find a scrap of memory worth saving after a fire. Snacks of buttered bread (vegan margarine on rye) and Chocolate Macadamia Nut Cookies gave us energy for the endeavor.

Most people's typical Christmas experiences include extravagant spending, a flurry of gift wrap, and a large dead animal on the table. Often vegans are environmentally conscious so discuss the holiday ahead of time. Maybe there are presents to share that do not waste wrapping paper as well as a suitable menu to be found.

I prefer Christmas to be a time to reflect and explore together. A Christmas hike in the woods with someone special wins my heart over a mound of presents. When I have been in relationships where gifts were the norm, especially with children, I took the time to make meaningful presents involving the children. Planning and making gifts from the heart makes Christmas into a season, not just a day. The memories last a lifetime.

Thanksgiving

Thanksgiving for many vegans is an awkward holiday because of the food—the big dead turkey who did not ask to be the center of attention. If a vegan is at a traditional gathering, many of the side dishes can have vegan or nonvegan ingredients: cranberry sauce, sweet potatoes, mashed potatoes, green beans, corn, bread, cornbread, squash, apple pie, and pumpkin pie. Depending on where the event takes place, the host could be informed of the vegan attendee and adjust recipes, the vegan could offer to help in the kitchen, or the vegan could offer to bring food to share. Nevertheless any gathering should be more about people than food.

Dinshah Thanksgiving has always been my favorite holiday. Usually forty to fifty of my relatives gather at my mom's place. Some of the people are not vegan, but all the potluck dishes are required to be vegan. We assemble for a group photo and then we eat an afternoon dinner. We play games until someone decides it is time for the evening dessert extravaganza, so many vegan desserts they warrant their own separate meal.

Dinshah Thanksgiving would be a great place to take a nonvegan man who was serious about me. Imagine having the opportunity to sample fifty vegan dishes! He might have to endure a multitude of questions from well-meaning relatives, but it would be an experience he would never forget...and hopefully look forward to every year.

One year when I wasn't able to make it to Dinshah Thanksgiving, I was invited to celebrate with Dude and Barb, a vegan and nonvegan couple (p. 147). Barb loves to cook and made two equally impressive meals, vegan for Dude and me, traditional for Barb and her brother.

If you want to celebrate a vegan Thanksgiving, but don't have vegan relatives or friends, look into local vegetarian groups that may be gathering. Often these gatherings take place near, but not on that Thursday. Holidays can be celebrated on whatever day one chooses. Perhaps you could start a vegan gathering with a few friends on the Saturday two days after the official holiday.

Easter

I have great Easter memories. Some involve making vegan treats for friends. Some involve the Easter bunnies (my companion rabbits) delivering the treats. Occasionally I wander into a church as I think that is what the holiday is supposed to remind us to do.

This year I had a memorable Easter with three nonvegans. Oliver invited me to dinner with his friends. We made Hidden Treasure Peppers, a hearty potato and pepper dish in a flaky phyllo crust, to offer at the gathering. On the trip across town, Oliver asked if he should explain to his friends that it was a vegan dish. I said I prefer just to blend in; just tell them it's a pepper casserole, unless they ask for more specifics.

We arrived at Mary and Mick's house to an overwhelming welcome by seven dogs, who thankfully were quickly escorted into the backyard. Mary was putting finishing touches on everything. I cringed as she pre-buttered all the vegetables, but decided this was definitely going to be one of those "build bridges" days. Other than the ham, everything else was squarely vegetarian and mostly vegan: salad, corn, green beans, rolls, roasted potatoes, and blackberry pie...all delicious. Mick liked my casserole so much he not only complimented it at the table, but eagerly accepted leftovers for his lunch the next day. I never told him it was vegan.

Birthdays

Cake and ice cream are associated with birthdays. For vegans, there are two options: make new traditions that center around other foods and activities or find vegan cake and ice cream. Terrific recipes exist for vegan cakes. Fran Costigan has entire books devoted to vegan desserts, including *More Great Good Dairy-Free Desserts Naturally*. Some cities have vegan bakeries that can bake you a cake to order. Nondairy ice cream is easy to find in most supermarkets. This could be a good opportunity to explore something new together if the birthday person is not vegan, but in a relationship with a vegan.

Fourth of July and other summer gatherings

Summer gatherings are synonymous with meat on the grill. Bring veggie burgers or veggie dogs. If the thought of them cooking on the same grill as meat is offensive, take vegan options out of their plastic wrap and put them in aluminum foil before grilling.

I recently attended a picnic where the host was thoughtful to have two separate grills, one devoted to exclusively vegan products. The veggie burgers were taking a long time to cook so I went over and chatted up the grillmaster. He confided that he had no idea how to cook a veggie burger and was concerned they might not be getting cooked enough. Many burgers were already horribly blackened to hard crunchy charcoal.

"These are perfect," I said, pointing to a newer cluster of burgers on the grill. "Veggie burgers just need to be heated to a pleasant temperature, lightly browned with a few grill marks. There's no danger of sickness like there'd be from eating uncooked meat."

The veggie dogs were done and he was happy to toss two of those on my plate. "They don't look done to me. They didn't change any," he said.

"Yes, I have eaten these straight from the can, but they are better warm from the grill. They're delicious. Thank you."

I went to a neighborhood picnic with Hank last summer and he commented that most items were "salads" of pasta or potatoes disgustingly drowned in mayonnaise. The bean salads tragically looked more like soup; the extra dressing could be drained off, but pickled beans do not taste like much. Most of the things were surprisingly not appetizing to Hank's nonvegan palate. Perhaps he had gotten too used to my cooking.

Try making a potato salad with just a hint of soy mayonnaise or light vinaigrette. Fruit salad needs no dressing. Platters of fresh cut fruit are a favorite. Make a salad using fresh garden vegetables and add some canned beans for a nice touch of hearty flavor. Keep a healthy dressing on the side so the lettuce does not wilt. Late-summer tomato and basil salads are amazing fresh from the garden. Roasted vegetables are easy to make; either use the recipe on page

56 or cook them on a grill. Opportunities abound to show off the fresh flavors of great summer vegan foods.

Romantic picnics

In a picturesque park, two people sit on a picnic blanket by a stream. They open their picnic basket and inside they find any combination of the following:

Pita bread, raw veggie sticks (carrot, celery, broccoli, cauliflower, radish), hummus
Bucket of watermelon chunks
Grapes or cherries to feed each other
Any other fruit or fruit salad
Vegan takeout
Cold vegan pizza
Ingredients for build-your-own subs——whole wheat French bread sliced sub-style, avocado, sliced tomatoes and olives, stir-fried spinach and mushrooms, secret sauce (vegan mayonnaise with hot sauce). Subs can be premade if you know what people like and you're certain the subs will be eaten soon.
Nut butter and jelly sandwiches
Cookies or muffins
Any leftovers that can be easily transported
Beverages
Always have bottles of water, napkins, and any necessary utensils.

Potlucks

Plan on bringing a vegan main dish such as Jeff Eight Veggie Stew or Paul's Portobello Potatoes that is so great it could satisfy someone as a one-dish meal, just in case it is the only vegan choice at dinner. If you know ahead of time that others will definitely bring vegan options, coordinate efforts for a main dish, side dish, and dessert. If it is an entirely vegan potluck, the vegan should be happy, yet sensitive to the nonvegan and give suggestions for what the nonvegan date might enjoy. Nonvegans should try a tiny sample of each unfamiliar vegan thing; then go back for seconds of what they like.

Work parties

These are a bit like potlucks, but it is more important to bring something that makes a great impression. If you are vegan, being well fed is secondary to impressing others with your best dish. Bring a dish that wowed nonvegans in the past, not a new recipe.

If you are not a vegan but have a vegan co-worker, making the extra effort to provide something vegan is appreciated. Make sure to casually mention to the vegan person that the dish is vegan, or bring the recipe and place it by the dish. The vegan will be grateful for your concerned efforts.

Hank (p. 47) adds music to the menu to make any occasion special.

Dating Vegans

Inviting Multiple Nonvegan Guests
to a Vegan Dinner

The basic principles here are the same as inviting one nonvegan person, ask for allergies or food sensitivities. Depending on the size of the group ask some of them for favorite vegetables and type of preferred dessert. Review "How to Create Vegan Meals Loved by Meat-eating Dates" (p. 23). Dinners for nonvegan guests generally fall into three categories: survive, impress, and influence.

Survive: These guests are not interested in veganism at all, but there is a good reason for their invitation to dinner. They may be future in-laws, a boss, or others. They will probably never change their diet, but it would be nice to survive the meal without too much ridicule. Sometimes this type may arrive in survival category, but leave impressed.

For the "survival" guests avoid vegan stereotypes: forget the salad unless you know they like salad. Hide the tofu in planning to make vegan versions of common foods; either make tofu undetectable or don't use it. Stay away from anything that would be considered weird, such as couscous or kombu. Try pasta or potato dishes, vegetable stew, chips and dips, rice and vegetables, or portobello mushrooms. Take familiar vegetables and grains and prepare them in a tasty new way. They will be surprised at how vibrant, colorful, delicious, and easy a healthy vegan main dish can be! Suggestions: Paul's Portobello Potatoes or Hidden Treasure Peppers with a dessert of Takedown Chocolate Brownies or Pineapple Upside Down Cake.

Impress: Some guests arrive open-minded, interested in learning about being vegan, and eager to try new dishes. These people may often be friends or neighbors. If they are impressed enough, they may leave influenced.

For the "impress" guests it is good to include some unique, innovative, or uncommon items along with the more common foods. They may be excited to learn about interesting grains or tofu dishes. If it is their second or third visit give them *Dating Vegans, Healthy Hearty Helpings,* or *The 4-Ingredient Vegan* ahead of time and let them pick recipes. Or ask what type of food they would like to try and give them a couple of choices. Often the discussion at one meal will lead to the menu ideas for the next occasion.

Influence: Guests who are most willing to enjoy a vegan dinner are often kids, health-conscious adults, or dates. It is a great opportunity for them to learn about healthy choices and compassion.

The menu should be primarily foods that are easy, tasty, and fun to make such as pizza, desserts, and smoothies. Let the guests help make it. Be prepared for it to take longer than if you cooked by yourself! Kids love to try things they make, develop a sense of pride at learning to create a meal, and (with proper guidance) can be a great help in getting dinner prepared. When cooking with other people's kids, be careful to respect their parents' views while introducing new ideas. Serve Philip's Blue Chocolate Dessert and "Chocolate" Zucchini with popular easy favorites such as corn on the cob and veggie pizza.

One of my favorite easy recipes for kids (or a date who does not cook, but wants to learn) is Mix-It-Up Pizza and Dip. Just mix canned refried beans in a bowl with an equal amount (or less) of pasta sauce or tomato sauce. Hot sauce to taste and a hint of water also work if tomato sauce is not available. The bean sauce should be easily spreadable yet thick. Add favorite ingredients such as chopped spinach, corn kernels, grated carrots, sliced mushrooms, or pitted olives. Mix together and spread thickly on the cut side of bagel halves or sturdy bread, placing them bean-side-up on a baking sheet. Bake a few minutes until the bagels are lightly toasted. As they bake, break out a bag of tortilla chips; use extra bean mix for dip.

This simple pizza has been so well received that my friend Woj, an avid hunter who eats venison daily, set aside his venison stew to share a vegan meal with me when I helped him work on his board and batten garage siding. A few Oatmeal Raisin Cookies completed his pleasure.

Todd, my Texan friend who eats stereotypical Texas fare, said of the same can't-miss meal, "I didn't know what to expect with the pizza, but it tasted good. I would definitely request it again! The cookies were delicious. I'll request this meal again next time we visit."

Steve, who never ever cooks, let me help him make the pizza in his kitchen and is actually considering doing it by himself. He might make the dip for the next party with his colleagues.

The Watkins (p. 144) frequently dine with mixed-eating company.

Vegan Issues to Discuss
for a Long-term Relationship

Questions to ask:

Food: Would there be a vegan kitchen? What concessions would be made? What would you be willing to change? Try? How much do you eat together? What are you not able to give up? Or would be difficult to give up? What personal habits may be offensive to the vegan if the nonvegan continues to eat animal products, and how can that be remedied (e.g. brush teeth, shower after barbequing meat)?

Non-food items: Do you have nonvegan items (leather, wool, silk, feathers, fur)? Would you keep them? Donate them? Use them until they wear out? Replace with vegan when possible? Buy what like/need regardless of source?

Kids: Would they be raised vegan? Would they eat vegan food at home? Would they see a parent eat nonvegan food? What choices do they have and what information would they receive? What if there are kids already? Would they be expected to adjust? Would choices be explained and supported by both parents? What would each parent explain?

Social settings: What is each person comfortable with? Are both people vegan all the time? Should the nonvegan person eat animal products with friends and family?

Other topics: What does each person know about being vegan and from what perspective: health, ethics, and environment? About which areas would it be good to learn more? How? Watch videos? Attend a conference? Go to a local vegetarian group? Would you go apple-picking together? Tour a slaughterhouse?

What issues are related to veganism, but not essentially vegan? Are there environmental and health concerns such as voluntary simplicity, organic food, recycling, health care and immunizations, vehicle options, or where to live?

Exploring Compatibility Issues (with Oliver)

Numbers are predictable, people are not.

Over the course of a few weeks, when Oliver and I hung out together, I asked many questions that we would have had to resolve if we had continued to progress in a serious long-term relationship. Perhaps I was more at ease with him as a friend than if we were pressured by contemplating being together forever, but we enjoyed each other's company and hope the transcriptions of some of our conversations are helpful to people exploring vegan issues.

Leather

Oliver arrived promptly at half past five looking like he just stepped off the page of *GQ, Men's Health,* or *Outdoors.* Whichever magazine, I wanted a copy. A gray t-shirt hugged his solid chest under a fine tan short-sleeve button-down shirt. His favorite Polo jeans took over from under his shirttails and led their way to leather boots that could serve equally well for construction or hiking. He strode purposefully to my front door. I suspended my thoughts about cowhide footwear and welcomed him.

Later I spotted his dog tag from his time in the marines attached to a bootlace and tucked in unobtrusively. He granted me permission to investigate. Claypool OJ, A neg, social security #, USMC, M, Christian. I rescinded my aversion and decided these are the leather boots I would never want him to give up to become vegan because they must have miles of memories and be durable enough to create mountains more.

Trapping

Oliver and I needed to explore beyond the comfort of predictable "dinner and movie" experiences. We planned a weekend vacation adventure at my cabin. I was guessing the odds of whether we would actually go as I sensed his hesitation despite his interest in camping and adventures. I did not know if it was the city boy in him, the uniqueness of outdoor showering facilities, the promise of coyotes howling, many mysterious all-vegan meals, or the long number of continuous hours with me that scared him the most.

We shared the driving responsibility for Betsy, his black 2007 Pontiac G6, a practical yet sporty car despite being automatic. Betsy liked to go faster than I do and I had to keep scanning the speedometer. Concentrating on the road, I occasionally caught glimpses of Oliver napping as I checked traffic on the right to change lanes. Being trapped in a car together provides a good forum for meaningful discussion; however, picking the right moment is essential. Sleepy was not the right mode, but the weekend would provide other opportunities.

Being trapped in a car can also be a metaphor for being trapped in a trap if one needs a venue for bringing up trapping for sport or fur. In a conversation at the cabin we both admitted that we have been trappers…of mice. My traps were the live, catch-n-release-elsewhere type. His were the more classic mousetrap with a definitive end. We agreed that sometimes a few mice must die to keep hundreds more from being born and overrunning one's house. I would be offended if he were going outside and setting traps for creatures, which he does not do.

A few days after our trip a mouse jumped out of the sleeve of my favorite vinyl motorcycle coat with faux-leopard interior after it hung in the shed at work for two short hours. As I saw the shredded remnants of the sleeve lining that had taken the form of a nest and uttered a few words of profanity, I better understood his point about trapping to kill the cute black-beady-eyed critters.

Levels of compassion

For meals on our cabin trip I served mostly simple things that did not require recipes or much forethought, vegan camping food for the nonvegan man. Fresh strawberries, cashew butter and strawberry jelly sandwiches, artichoke and roasted red pepper dip (simply blended) served with pita and tortilla chips, trail mix, stewed lentils with various greens and herbs, and baked potatoes. More elaborate than a backpacker's meal, yet this food was easy to fix in my cabin. I had also packed a large stash of Oatmeal Raisin Cookies, which he knew where to find. We agreed everything tastes better outdoors.

We hiked my woods in the 75-degree sunshine, and took our laptops outside for the working section of our "writers' retreat." Our power cords stretched from the outdoor outlet in opposite directions and perhaps our thoughts were distant too.

"These clouds look like God's cigarette smoke floating by," he said.

As he slapped at bugs I asked, "Are we living in the ashtray?"

"I'm an optimist," he said as he went to investigate a strange knot formation in the top of a tree. He seemed more relaxed as he adjusted to his fourteenth hour at the cabin.

In my estimation of Oliver's 9-to-5 accounting world, numbers are logical. They can be added vertically and horizontally with linear interpretation, predictability. One of his favorite leisure activities is lifting weights, where the numerically selected plates travel vertically. He returned and asked what I was writing. I divulged a tentative title, "Numbers are predictable; I am not."

He retorted, "People are predictable with preset emotional responses. Numbers are random." I resolved to test his response theory with some vegan issues soon.

On the return trip clever Oliver said he is an open book. I asked him to read me page 63. "Page intentionally left blank," he said.

I decided to send a few bugs in his direction and determine the extent of his preset emotional responses and depth of his compassion by asking, "What would happen if a ____ walked into the cabin?" I inserted different creatures with the same question: mosquito, fly, cricket, spider, frog, mouse, rat, chipmunk, squirrel, dog, deer, chicken, turkey, and cow.

The summary of his responses concluded that frog, dog, chipmunk, and squirrel live. Those who would die at his hand include mouse, spider, cricket, and rat. "A mouse doesn't wander in. Mouse invades. Same as a rat. Rats bite people. People die from plague."

"Chicken?" I asked.

"Would be lunch. No, I'd shoo it out."

"Turkey?" I inquired.

"Turkey is the same as chicken, I'd help it out."

"Cow?"

"Cow. I'd help it out"

"Do you realize what I'm setting you up for?"

"Bear, coyote?"

"No. Instead of my cabin a chicken walked into the supermarket," I posed.

"All the same rules apply except technically I'm not sleeping in the supermarket, but I am at the cabin."

"What if the chicken couldn't walk in?"

"On display being sold? I think he'd be beyond my help at that point," he said.

"Maybe that particular chicken, but…"

"There's nothing I can do for him because he's dead. I could buy him. Maybe not. People have to survive."

"Yes, but there are plenty of things in the other aisles."

"Usually I buy from the other aisles, but if my friends want turkey meat I'd accommodate."

"Ever watch movies of animals being killed?"

"Yes. Chickens getting their heads cut off, cows getting slaughtered. It was gruesome."

"Do you ever think about that when you eat meat?"

"Maybe a little bit. I guess I thank God for providing me the food that I eat. And sometimes I thank the animal."

"Do you like the taste?"

"Usually it's pretty good. I never crave the taste."

"Any chance you'd give up meat?"

"I don't eat meat too often. There's always something that might convince me."

That was far enough for the conversation to go as we rolled down my street, a good place to take a break. Had we had a few more hours in the car, I could have pushed this line of questions too far. It is important to know where someone else draws the line and what I can tolerate. His enthusiasm for bug-squishing in the country was not the gate for a bigger demon. I had carried a spider outside that he would have squished, but found it futile to escort the moth because even turning off the light, two moths flew in for every one that flew out. He smacked the moth easily and we both definitely slap mosquitoes.

I had the future opening that there may be something to convince him to quit meat and he reconfirmed he does not eat it much. As he carried my bag to the door, I asked if we could continue the conversation another time. He was agreeable to picking it up with "What about milk?"

Dairy Discussion

A few days later, reclining on my brown cotton canvas picnic blanket on the unmown grass beyond a lively stream in Glen Echo Park in Columbus, we resumed our conversation. We shared avocado-veggie subs, fresh cherries, and Peach-Oatmeal Muffins as the clouds began to drift together as a big frothy milk sea. "Tell me about milk."

"Giving up milk would be difficult. I like yogurt. I eat it with fruit. Soy yogurt is different. Like soy ice cream is different. It has a bit of a funny soy taste. Soy yogurt is okay. It's like offering someone fruit that was frozen and thawed or fresh fruit. My taste likes fresh. It's all about the taste. There's price too. And what one's used to. Cheese is good every now and then. I love lasagna.

115

If you made lasagna without cheese, but was just as good, that would be fine with me."

I thanked him for giving me a lasagna challenge and knew I could perfect a lasagna to his liking. (Oliver's Spinach Strata, p. 86) I also made a mental note to serve him my preferred brand of soy yogurt and various nondairy ice creams such as a decadent chocolate-based flavor. Both proved more successful for his tastes.

"Is milk your favorite drink?" I asked as I recalled last time I looked in his fridge: two gallons of milk, a dozen eggs, some strawberries, and a typical bachelor assortment of condiments.

"I drink whole milk, but I like juice best. Apple cider is my favorite. Eggnog I can do without. Usually I just drink milk. I've done without it too, to see the difference, if there were any effects on my overall health, how I look, feel, and work. I didn't notice a difference."

"Did you discern anything about how milk products can be responsible for more mucus?"

"The mucus thing is definitely true," he said, surprising me with his response. I could have left it at that but decided he could handle a bit more on this topic.

We discussed dairy calves and he was already aware of the males becoming veal. "Do you eat veal?"

"I've tried it. …doesn't taste as good as some other meats. … and it is baby."

"Does that make a difference?"

"I suppose."

I knew he does not eat meat often so I returned to the milk ethics. "Do you know how they make the cows give milk constantly?"

"They keep them pregnant somehow."

"Yes. It's rape."

He looked perplexed as I continued, "People rape them; they put their arm in and deposit semen robbed from a bull. As soon as a cow gives birth, the calf is taken away. The cow is raped again. The cycle continues."

Oliver asked if I was certain. I had definitely hit on a fact he did not know, and perhaps hit on a nerve. I let him digest the information with his last bite of muffin. I silently leaned back into the hillside and searched for anomalies in the vast ocean of opaque sky. He nuzzled closer and let out a soft, kind, gentle low, "Moooo."

Reaffirming cow compassion

The next day I sent the following email:

Oliver,

You seemed surprised at the information that cows are raped. Scientifically speaking, cows are routinely artificially inseminated. A person forcibly inserts his arm into the cow's rectum to position the cow's uterus. Then a metal insemination rod is thrust into her vagina and up to the cervix. The farmers in the industry call the cage where this is performed the "rape rack."

I found a video on YouTube called "Happy Cows - Behind the Myths." It's kinda long at 6:36 or 8:31, but if you watch the 6:36 version for a minute from 1:28 to 2:28 it shows a diagram of the insemination process and a rape rack.

Moo!

Anne

The next week during a westward travel together, I had the opportunity to discuss happy cows. He confirmed watching the video and commented, "Some of the dairy farmers claimed it was biased. They take care of the cows. The cows don't mind being milked."

"Was that in the video?"

"I read it in the posted comments."

"Do you have a comment to post for me?"

"My opinion is to treat animals as humanely as possible."

I did not pressure him to expand on the definition of "humanely as possible," as I could sense his interest in discussing the topic was setting quicker than the sun that evening.

Chicken seeds

Another food talk surfaced when we were gardening together, or replacing some weeds with seeds in his backyard. Since we were on the seed topic, I began with, "Are you an avid egg eater?" I had never seen Oliver eat an egg since he eats vegan food when we are together even if he fixes the meal.

"Oh yeah, fry them, scramble them, anyway I can. Put in lasagna, pie, baked goods, full of nutrients."

"Are you okay with eating a chicken's period?"

"Yes."

"Does it bother you how the chickens are kept in their factory farmed cages? Beaks cut, crammed together in tiny cages."

"I'm not sure how they feel. I've seen a bit of film on it. The eggs roll away on conveyors."

I could have continued on the cruelties involved with layer hens, but sensed I should keep the conversation a bit lighter especially since he claimed to be familiar with the process. His attention was distracted as he was trying to swat a carpenter bee that was invading his woodshed. I made a mental note to crack him on eggs later.

Babies

The following weekend we shared a ride to New York City where we individually visited our respective friends. I wanted to resume our chicken talk and tell him that to create layer hens, some of the eggs must fertilize and hatch. Half of those adorable fuzzy chicks would be of his gender, and would be automatically tossed in a garbage can to suffocate.

Instead I chose a different path to peck. I wondered what it would be like on the other side of the fence. What concerns would a typical animal-products consumer have about dating a vegan?

I reclined my seat to get a better look at the soy yogurt clouds swirled across the blueberry smoothie sky above the spring green deciduous arbors that delighted the cantankerous Allegheny Mountains. "IF you were in a long-term relationship, what concerns would you have about dating a vegan?"

"None," he said. At that moment I hated this perfectly compatible-for-me answer, delivered with complete honesty from my friend who said he did not feel chemistry for me. We had six more hours of our ride together and had already played guessing games of a typical travel nature and read medical stories to each other from his library book. I decided to prompt him with some potential situations and see if I could arouse any potential difficulties.

"What if you had kids?" I asked, jumping right into what I figured would be one of the most serious topics.

"I would be concerned in the gestation period that a baby would be getting enough nutrients to develop well: protein, B12, calcium..."

We talked about beans and nuts for protein, nutritional yeast and fortified soymilk as sources of B12, and the bounty of leafy greens that provide calcium. I told him a vegan woman's commitment to variety in food consumption would take care of getting proper nutrients and could be confirmed by her doctor.

"So would you let your kids be raised vegan if scientific data supported veganism to be healthy for them?"

"Yes, if my wife wanted to maintain a vegan household, I would support that choice. However, I would want my kids to ultimately decide for themselves, as every person should be able to do. Hopefully we would be able to explain to the kids both sides of the story—why people are vegan and why people are not vegan."

Ethics, health, or environment

"People become vegan for ethical, health, or environmental reasons; which is more likely to appeal to you?"

"I suppose environmental or ethical." His answer surprised me because he tends to be a heath-conscious eater. We talked about how it is quite possible to be a junk-food vegan. I liked his ethical-related answer because that is the perspective that calls to me most.

Life is not about agreeing on everything. It is a process of learning and respecting the other person. Complete agreement on all issues, even the vegan issues, might extinguish a spark. It should be acknowledged that on some issues opposites may attract. Meaningful dialogue is about finding what opinions are shared, when to agree to disagree, and what can become a good debate.

Occasionally when I brought up vegan ethics topics, I reminded Oliver that I am not trying to convert him, just trying to understand his views. And if he did not like a line of questioning, we did not have to go there. I always tried to be sensitive when I provided him with unfamiliar information. I was also well aware that he is intelligent, compassionate, an avid reader, and a lifelong consumer of animal products.

Numbers are predictable or random depending on the situation. We agree to disagree and both of us can be correct. His answers to vegan issues were similarly predictable at times, unpredictable at other times. Again we were both correct. I decided to keep the title of this section and expand it completely to the plural: "Numbers are Predictable, People are Not," fully knowing that on both fronts we shared opinions and provided debate. He hated the title and advocated its reversal. I made it the subtitle instead.

Pillow talk

"What if you unknowingly offended a vegan person, say brought home a great fluffy pillow, but it was full of feathers?"

"I'd return it," Oliver said without hesitation.

"Why not stand up for your right to have the pillow you want?"

"It's a pillow. What do I care? From an emotional standpoint the vegan has emotions she cannot change, whereas my emotions to the pillow are not there. So it's easy for me to put the other person's emotions ahead of my own."

"Is there a time that your emotions would come first on an issue of vegan ethics?"

"I don't think so."

"Say your relationship broke up, would you go back to not being vegan?" I have appreciated that he extends his compassion to our friendship when we spend time together. He makes a conscious choice to respect and understand my beliefs. He makes it seem so easy that I often forget he is not vegan.

"Yes. Otherwise I'd be vegan already if I had motivation for it," he said. This allowed me to deduce that partly he had not been exposed to enough reasons to be vegan, nor has he encountered a catalyst for finding them. This, I reminded myself, is not my role with him.

"So of environmental, health, or ethical reasons for being vegan, you would actually just add the choice to pick relationship reasons?"

"Yes."

"Why not make the vegan person compromise for the relationship?"

"Because she has emotions regarding the matter, where as I do not. It's not going to make any difference to me. It is good for her to accept me for who I am, but when emotions are involved, relationships are about compromise. What you eat does not define who you are. You can change without compromising your core values, your integrity."

"So what are your core values? What defines you?"

"Compassion, passion, honesty, loyalty, adventure, cleanliness, and good health."

I loved the thoughtful consistency in his answers and the earnestness in which he listed his values, so similar to mine. He could be an ideal mate for a vegan. Oliver had provided terrific answers I never dreamed to find. Yet compatibility does not equal chemistry.

Getting the boot

The Pennsylvania scenery looked different around each swerve of the turnpike, yet still the same, a canvas painted in spring green lower section with an upper of bright blue and white. We rolled into a rest stop to stretch our legs and I could walk another mile in his shoes. "What if you bought vegan boots and they were not as comfortable as your boots with the dog tag? Let's say you got a terrible blister."

"In some circumstances like if a vegan boot causes blisters and my leather boots do not, then my comfort should be a priority."

"Ah ha. So you would put yourself first. Good. I was beginning to wonder about you. I wouldn't want you to be getting walked on in a relationship."

Cheating

"What about the actions you take when the vegan is not around? Could you put yourself first then?" I had never gotten the feeling that Oliver was spineless or uncertain about his own principles, but I kept probing.

"If she felt like I was letting her down if I ate animal products when I was not around her, then I would avoid it if I were in a relationship. However, anything that affects my health in a negative way, I would take a stand against. Being a vegan might affect my health in a negative way like finding enough protein or getting less vitamins. I don't know the long-term effects. Maybe I should see a study of vegans versus nonvegans and the health effects on their lives."

I have every confidence that an intelligent eater like Oliver would be able to find a bounty of vegan variety, perhaps with a little friendly guidance for the protein and vitamins. Information such as *The China Study* by T. Colin Campbell could quell his fears. "So scientific evidence would be important to you?"

"Yes."

When Oliver suggested reading to each other as a good pastime for our journey, I divulged that I had brought a book I had been reading; *The Engine 2 Diet* by Rip Esselstyn. We took turns driving and reading aloud. I read the chapter "Crazy Myths About Food" and Oliver read "The Medical Proof Behind the Engine 2 Diet."

The book outlines how and why to eat plant-strong (vegan) in an easy-to-follow four-week program to focus on losing weight, becoming physically fit, or reducing risk of disease. The absence of calorie-counting or portion control makes this diet appeal to many people. It is very clear about what to eat (plants) and what not to eat (animals). The diet works for losing weight and lowering cho-lesterol when a person begins from a standard American diet laden with animal products.

Esselstyn hit on some of Oliver's concerns about protein, B12, and calcium, but Oliver was reluctant to agree he had learned something. I did not press the issue. I decided to let him chew on it, along with the bean burritos he suggested I order veganized for us.

Calories

One day when Oliver and I were preparing a meal together, he asked about getting enough calories, or more specifically, my opin-ion on how to add more calories of a healthy variety. Later I thought it would be helpful to write down the suggestions so I included the following in an email:

"All the following are generally healthy higher-calorie foods: beans, whole grains, nuts, dried fruits, granola, trail mix, shakes (with soymilk, fruit, nuts, flaxseeds), burritos, bagels, decadent desserts (homemade or from a trusted source so not 'bad' for you, just good calories), nut butter in or on things, avocado, olives, soynuts, seeds such as sesame or sunflower (make sure they are well-chewed so they get digested), tempeh, and more. Remember variety and moderation. More importantly guide from how you feel. (Are you full of energy? satisfied with meals? generally healthy and happy?)"

The next week we had a high-calorie picnic lunch with avocado subs and muffins. I brought along trail mix for our hike. He ate more than I did that day.

Oliver does not like nut chunks in desserts, but whole nuts are a good snack. Although the day I made him Chocolate Macadamia Nut Cookies with and without nuts, he decided he liked both so he may be rescinding his nutty opinion.

A couple of weeks after our calorie conversation Oliver went food shopping, arriving home at the same time that he had invited me to share leftover Oliver's Spinach Strata for dinner. I respect his privacy and decisions so I did not look at what was in his bags. A comical explosion of his key ring at the door required my assistance to find the missing front door key that landed in a bag of curious groceries. Oliver explained that he purchased five pounds of almonds and walnuts, "I bought more nuts today than I have in all my combined nut purchases before now," as he sampled some from each bag. "I think I like pecans better than walnuts."

"Why are you suddenly investing in the nut market?"

"I want to make sure I eat enough healthy calories," replied my favorite investment accountant.

It is common for people to worry about getting enough protein although most Americans get too much. Many men would have robotically picked up meat from the supermarket. Oliver wisely chose nuts.

This part of the book came together easily because Oliver is an Oliver, a genuine nice guy, and we remain great friends.

Compatibility Conversations with More Meat-eating Men

Conversations about vegan issues may not go so smoothly for those of us without an Oliver. I wondered if Oliver had set me up for disappointment in future relationships. Could I ever find both compatibility and chemistry with an intelligent, healthy, athletic, compassionate man who understands my emotions?

I thought about my past serious relationships. Former-husband Dude Hamre and I remain good friends. He had become vegan because health and animal rights issues made sense to him when I shared information with him. I asked him recently about his continued commitment to being vegan (p. 147). He said, "Lovin' the creatures, man."

Only two of my other serious relationships were vegan when I met them. Most of my male friends and dates are (or were) not vegan, but enjoy my cooking as much as I enjoy cooking for or with them. I have never become seriously involved with someone who was absolutely wonderful, except completely anti-vegan. To gain more perspective on vegan issues options, I conversed with three of my dates who I thought would be the least likely to change their lifestyle to accommodate a vegan mate. I asked each of them, **"What would be the hardest thing about dating a vegan, especially if dating progressed into a long-term relationship?"**

Robert Crane

For Robert the hardest thing about dating a vegan depends on whether she would require him to change his own dietary habits. If not, then the worry of accidentally forgetting to read a label for her properly when grocery shopping would be his primary ongoing concern. Another concern would be thinking something is vegan and finding out it is not.

If he did need to change his eating to match hers, "That would mean I'd have to give up bacon."

"Yes, what's special about bacon?" I asked.

"You don't understand. You're vegan. It's bacon!" he said, sounding humorously like a cartoon dog on a television advertisement. "Bacon is God." He referred to the taste. "I could always give something up, but bacon would be the hardest to give up."

"Would you expect her to compromise some? Why?"

"In any relationship there should be compromise. That's just fair. If all the decisions are one-sided then the relationship is one-sided. You could never force someone to do something anyway. It has to be because they want to. However the two people work it out. I'd trade bacon for some type of non-food negotiation." We decided to censor out his hypothetical examples of what he would be willing to bargain. "It would completely depend on the dynamic of the two people. Everything goes on the table for discussion in a long term relationship."

Brad Holdren

"In my imagination the hardest thing about dating a vegan is the inevitable, 'Where are we going to eat, Honey?' Of course I'd want somewhere with meat and she needs options too." Brad did not think navigating restaurants would be too hard, but quickly thought of another difficulty, the grocery store. "I would have to hear, 'You're not going to put that in the cart.' and all the lectures about the dead animal selection."

I refrained from telling him that he would probably not be allowed to call his vegan partner "Honey." "So you would each maintain your own ways, one a meat-eater and the other a vegan?"

"I would say in any long-term relationship it's about sharing two lives, not about blending into one. Blending inevitably happens. I'm gonna be eating some vegan dishes. As long as I can still eat meat it's okay. If that type of thinking becomes an issue, then it probably won't be a long-term relationship."

I told him about my vegan friend Jennie whose husband Dan has one specific meat drawer in the fridge and one specific pan to cook meat (p. 158). Brad would be okay with that arrangement.

Brad said, "The vegan gongs the meat-eater over the head with the pan and says, 'This is your pan.' He'll remember which pan to use. That part of the relationship stuff is easy."

Brad does not envision himself ever becoming vegan. We talked about a variety of related topics including vegansexuals, a term given to vegans who only date other vegans. We discussed taste, compatibility, compassion, and compromising.

"What about non-food items, like if you want silk sheets?" I tried to think of an example of something a couple would share.

"If there are certain sheets she wants, that's fine, as long as I get to sleep on them with her," Brad said. "Shows what I know about vegans, I didn't know there were other issues. I thought it was just about food."

"It includes not using animal products: leather, wool, silk, fur..."

"Any animal products...wow! I don't pay attention to what is animal or not. I don't think it would be a problem. I have enough problem finding made in the U.S.A. labels. Outside of the food, I can't think of anything made from animals that there aren't other options for."

We discussed leather shoes, the potential options of using what he has until they wear out or giving them away and now or later replacing with non-leather or continuing to use leather.

"If it's going to be a long-term relationship, I don't see the non-food vegan stuff being a problem. On the grand scale of 'squeezing the toothpaste' issues, vegan is not huge. Other topics like kids or religion seem tougher. I gotta believe it's just a learning process that involves cooperating together."

Brad said I posed concepts that deserved more thought. We agreed to talk again soon. I emailed what I had written thus far.

He replied, "I like this. The more I've thought about it and discussed it 'over cheeseburgers' with other friends I've come to the conclusion that it's really no more of an issue than anything else. Catholics and Jews marry each other. Canadians and Americans marry each other. Different races marry each other. Men and women have been marrying each other and we'll NEVER come close to compromising on the differences between men and women. The whole vegan issue is just one more piece of the ultimate puzzle of happiness."

Brad continued, "I can't imagine two people being in love and not being able to come to a compromise if one is a vegan. It's just such a small piece of the overall puzzle. It's amazing to me how many things in life we all make compromises on without thinking of them as hardships, yet when something we don't understand is introduced, we carry on like it's impossible. Very interesting!"

Dave Nagel

"I would worry about what she thought about me eating meat in front of her at the same table. I'd wonder if she thought negatively of me eating my hamburger or steak. I'd worry about whether it bothered her."

"Just ask her."

"Yes. We'd have to get that straightened out right off the bat."

"If it doesn't bother her, do you prepare two separate meals?

"Wow, that's a good question to consider. Hmm. What exactly is vegan again? Can a vegan cook meat?"

"I don't think she'd want to, but she could. I have one vegan friend who cooks meat for her husband." (p. 144)

"So that's possible?"

"Doubtful."

"I'd have to cook my own meat. Well, I do that anyway. No biggie. We could share salad, veggies, all that stuff. Fruit for dessert, nothing wrong with that."

"Now what if she said that you eating meat does bother her?"

"Can I eat it when she's not around? That's probably what I'd do, but I'd tell her, not sneak it. I'd be respectful of her, but honest.

I wouldn't want it to be a problem in a relationship. We'd have to talk it over. I don't think one person should change the philosophy of another. If they can't get along just because of that, then it's not much of a relationship. If they love each other, what they eat should not stand in the way of a good relationship."

Dave is planning to buy a motorcycle. I informed him that vegans object to leather. "Oh, I see. I don't have much leather, maybe shoes. Leather, like motorcycle jackets? What do vegans do?"

"Fake leather, synthetic."

"That would be okay. I'd wear that."

"What about animal products such as eggs, milk, and cheese? Would you be okay not having them in your house if she prefers?"

"Yah, that would be good. I would eat at a diner a couple times a week. I'd eat oatmeal, grits, and breakfast cereal at home. I guess there's soymilk. I could do that."

"Do your chickens make eggs you eat? What if she objected?"

"I'd sell 'em."

"Which would you sell first, the chickens or the eggs?"

"Both." Dave replied with a hearty laugh. "Till no more chickens here. It's about heartfelt love. What someone eats or wears shouldn't be a consideration. I think that's possible."

"Which is more likely: you adapting or her accepting you?"

"That's a good question."

"There's not a right or wrong answer." I am the only vegan Dave knows. "If you never meet another vegan you don't have to ever answer."

"You presented quite a scenario. She'd smell the hamburger with onions on my breath when I got home. I'd be like, 'Uh oh.' Busted. 'Please forgive me. I'll never eat another hamburger in my life'...and then I'd know the answer."

Information from Another Dating Vegan

Sometimes it is hard to admit, but not every guy wants to date ME. There are billions of other women on the planet and even the vegan ones may have entirely different opinions from mine. I decided to recruit some assistance from my friend, Maribeth Abrams, a lovely, talented, athletic nutritionist. Her fantastic new book, *The 4-Ingredient Vegan*, provides a wealth of simple recipes I highly recommend for luring the nonvegan mate to the table with minimal effort in the kitchen or amazing someone with vegan cooking skills when not a vegan. Maribeth shares my excitement for vegan food projects and we had fun collaborating on her four-ingredient book. She eagerly offered her opinions for exploring vegan issues…and opinions from two of her meat-eating dates.

Maribeth and Keith: Keith speaks openly about his admiration and respect for my veganism, especially as it pertains to health. Indeed, his own life path, encompassing athletics, martial arts, yoga and meditation, naturally leads to an increasingly pure diet. The more research he does, the more he believes that a whole foods vegan diet is optimal.

When it comes to matters of compassion and the environment, though, his opinions are less defined. For example, on the one hand he proclaims that he can't stand the thought of ground turkey, insisting that it just seems gross. But then one day I ran into him at Whole Foods scooping up the last few bites of chicken vindaloo. Having never seen him previously eat meat (he always eats vegan when we dine out), I was immediately brought back thinking about my pre-vegan roots when there were some foods I ate (e.g. chicken salad) and others that I didn't eat (e.g. chicken wings), knowing full well that my choices were based completely on emotion rather than logic.

Although he has yet to become vegan, Keith's diet has been gradually shifting from animal products toward whole, plant-based foods. Interestingly, although he embraces leather for furniture, car interiors, footwear and other common uses of cow skin, he touts his trail running shoes as vegan and in fact playfully flaunts this as a positive attribute. "Look Maribeth," he said, pointing to his well-used trail runners. "They're vegan!"

He acted surprised when I questioned their authenticity, explaining to him that not all running shoes are vegan no matter how synthetic they appear to be which is why I buy mine from a vegan store. However, the simple fact that he associates veganism with pride is delightful and even promising as a harbinger of a further developed relationship.

Keith, an accomplished athlete, is somewhat insistent that leather in running shoes is considered inferior because weather causes them to crack. That's why he is convinced that all high performance trail running shoes, including his, are vegan. Definitely something I should examine further.

Maribeth and Sam: Sam is a decidedly nonvegan guy, whom I dated for almost a year. Ironically, his lifestyle nearly encompassed veganism, minus the food part. He is environmentally conscious and proud of it. He never lets anything go to waste, watering his plants with collected rainwater or leftover water from the dog bowl. He composts. He hangs clothes up to dry. Sam is a builder and every wood scrap is always saved and used in some capacity whether integrating it into makeshift ski maintenance equipment, tucking it under the leg of a wobbly piece of furniture, or adding it to a wintertime fire. Sam embraces everything from washing out the occasional plastic bag to thinking up a hundred and one ways to re-use nearly every can and bottle that enters the household. He considers it his duty as a human being.

When it comes to saving precious land or water by cutting back on meat, he appears to think little of what leading environmentalists say: cutting back on animal products is the single most important thing that a human being can do to protect the environment.

I asked if he is bothered by the fact that his diet is equivalent to leaving the shower on all day, leaving a parked car running for hours on end, or turning on an air conditioner even though every window in the house is open.

Sam told me of starting up his lawnmower in early spring to find, to his horror, that a family of mice had been living underneath it and were now, suddenly, because of his action, in various stages of suffering and death. He could barely talk about it, including the part about how he decided to personally euthanize the suffering sentient beings as an alternative to their bleeding to death. It was deeply painful for him especially as he had caused their pain. His story was to show me that he too believes animals should be treated with compassion.

However, he actively supports factory farms, every day, by eating animal products. I pointed out that in eating those foods, he supports an industry that abuses, mutilates, tortures, and otherwise treats animals in a way that he clearly abhors. I reminded him that when it comes to the environment, the old adage "Real environmentalists don't eat meat." is inconveniently true.

"It's the way I'm used to eating," he said. "People like what they know; it makes them feel safe."

"You mean, like how slavery was in the South?"

"No. Not like slavery," he said, implying that factory farming does not even come close to slavery.

Too bad I never had the chance to show him a factory farm DVD, I thought to myself. Then he might equate animal agriculture with slavery, torture, and the most despicable abuse. And if we had had that opportunity, whether or not he decided to become vegan after viewing such an abomination wouldn't have been the important thing for me, at least at that moment. Rather, it would simply have been that he had become a witness.

For me, the important matter at hand when dating a nonvegan is how willing is that person to witness, to become available to the facts. Are they willing to witness for me? No one can become vegan for someone else. However, in my opinion, everyone is capable of witnessing factory farming if it is important to the person that he or she loves.

Nonvegans regularly ask vegans as to why they are vegan. But interestingly, the fascination goes both ways in that most vegans are equally curious as to why meat-eaters are meat-eaters.

Several months after Sam and I broke up we talked on the phone and I asked him if he would volunteer his insight for this book. He acquiesced and said that through our relationship, he had learned a lot about the reasons why people become vegan—in particular about how bad it is that humans are depleting the ocean.

I asked Sam what advice he would offer someone planning to date a vegan. "Be open-minded and get ready for an education."

Maribeth

Couples' Dating Success Stories and Favorite Recipes

These couples provide a banquet of ideas for relationships.

Long-Term Successful Relationships

So now let's check out some of my friends' relationships—those who are successful couples.

These couples have, either at the beginning of their relationship, somewhere during their dating, or at the current time, one person who is vegan and one person who is not vegan, or two people who evolved to vegan together. They display ingenuity and tolerance. Each couple divulges aspects of what has worked for them. They provide diverse opinions. Each shows that food choices, similar to other aspects of a relationship, do not have to divide a couple, but should be addressed. Ultimately it is both people in their entirety who need to be considered and accepted in a relationship.

I hope you find these couples as inspirational as I do.

The Great Persuader and the Gentle Decider

vegan (lifetime vegetarian) man + lifetime vegetarian woman =>

2 vegans

H. Jay Dinshah and Freya Dinshah

"Young man, American pacifist vegetarian, age 25, desires correspondence with young lady with view to marriage."

H. Jay Dinshah ran a personal ad in *Peace News*, a pacifist weekly newspaper published in London, England, with airmail copies distributed in the United States. At the time, Freya Smith and her mother sold *Peace News* in England outside Epsom railway station on Friday evenings. They read the paper, saw the ad, and thought it was kind of funny because it was unusual in those days to run such a personal ad. After several weeks of seeing the ad, Freya's mother felt sorry for Jay and suggested Freya write him so he would not think he was the only pacifist vegetarian out there.

Through their correspondence, which lasted over a year, Freya learned about Jay and his family. Freya visited Jay in July of 1960 after she had finished high school, as they wanted to see if they liked each other as much in person as they did in writing. The U.S. Embassy advised her to get a permanent visa as they thought she was likely to stay. They were right.

"We agreed on so many things in life and there were not a lot of vegetarians in those days. If we didn't get married we might regret missing the opportunity," Freya says of their decision to marry on August 1 1960.

Jay was vegan and had founded the American Vegan Society (AVS) in February 1960. Freya was vegetarian and became vegan over the course of corresponding with him. She gave up eggs first. Cheese was tougher to surrender.

Milk was difficult because good substitutes did not exist. Freya's mother mixed peanut butter and water in the blender. Freya was not fond of it, but recalls it was better than orange juice on cornflakes. Jay's mother made soymilk out of soy powder and water. Freya didn't think that tasted like much either.

It was a sacrifice to give up honey because Freya especially liked honey on toast. Molasses was a poor substitute. Many years later, she found rice syrup, which was better.

Shoes were hard to find without leather. Freya gradually found substitutes. She was excited when she found non-leather ice-skating boots.

From the beginning Jay and Freya shared a strong ethical connection. "He probably liked that I was young, impressionable, and by that time, vegan. I loved his mind, his ideas. He knew what he believed, what was right and wrong. I was still deciding what was practical while his code of ethics was all set. He was very honest about things. Peculiar thing was that he was right about things."

Jay had the confidence to be a renaissance man and a one-man-band—very efficient and an original thinker. When he got into something, he really got into it. Jay was eager to share his vegan message with everyone. The charismatic lecturer began by expressing himself well in writing articles for the *British Vegetarian Youth Movement* periodical and the *American Vegetarian-Hygienist* publication.

Freya had a lovely English rose complexion and naturally curly hair. Her kind demeanor and gentleness captured Jay's heart. Not a modern man with the house chores, Jay loved to play the piano and sing while Freya did the dishes.

"Jay loved cartoons," Freya shares. "We often went to the movies. Before the main feature there were cartoons such as Mickey Mouse or Donald Duck. He'd be laughing and rolling in the aisle. Me, I'd be thinking the poor creature got hurt."

"One of the first things Jay and I made together was banana ice cream." Simply whiz three bananas and 2/3 cup cashews in a blender. "We made it in the evening and put it in the freezer for the next day. It was his main contribution to the menu, although he could also bake potatoes."

Jay fixed his own midday meal that became affectionately referred to as "swill" years later by his children. "Swill" typically consisted of tomato juice, a can of corn, and a can of beans, mixed and heated, served on a bed of leftovers such as fried potatoes or on potato chips. "He didn't care whether I could cook or not. It didn't matter," Freya says. "What did matter was his healthy libido."

In the beginning of their marriage, Freya helped Jay's mother make meals for him and many of his seven siblings. A typical meal included rice, dal (yellow split peas with fried onions and curry powder), potatoes, green and yellow vegetables, lemonade, and cake or pie. Potato casserole was one of their favorite main dishes. Jay's mother made it with soy powder soymilk, which was acceptable in a casserole. Freya adapted it to Freya's Potato Casserole using corn milk. Jay asked for Potato Casserole every birthday and special occasion.

Jay and Freya went to live in California in 1962. Freya was collecting ideas for a cookbook, beginning with their mothers' recipes. During a cross-country lecture tour in 1961 she had picked up ideas from their various hosts. In 1965 she produced the landmark cookbook, *The Vegan Kitchen*, the first one in this country to use the word "vegan" in the title and the first to have an introduction giving the ethical reasons for eating vegan. Thirteen editions have been printed.

They returned to New Jersey and eventually moved into the old family homestead, which was too big for Jay's mother and sister, but began a new life as headquarters of AVS.

Jay and Freya attended the 1965 World Vegetarian Congress in Swanick, England. Jay spoke so dynamically he was invited by delegates of many nations to come to their countries to speak, particularly to India for the World Vegetarian Congress in 1967. Jay planned an around-the-world lecture tour to England, Ireland, Italy, Israel, India, Thailand, Malaysia, Indonesia, Australia, New Zealand, Hawaii, and west coast United States. He would leave after their first child was born. Jay's book *Song of India* is the collection of letters he wrote to baby Daniel, during his travels.

Freya and Jay did not have to find time to be together as most couples do, because they worked together every day. They shipped books, wrote *Ahimsa* magazine, put on conventions, had a second child (Anne), wrote books, and helped other people publish books. The couple shared a love of helping animals and spreading their vegan values. Their bond to each other, with vegan ethics at the core, inspired people. Their dedication and wisdom influenced many vegetarians and vegans to become actively involved in furthering vegetarianism and veganism. Vegan groundbreakers Jay and Freya were the first inductees into the Vegetarian Hall of Fame.

Freya and Jay

Dating Vegans

Freya's Potato Casserole

Yield: 4 servings

This Dinshah family favorite is popular with everyone. The recipe is from *The Vegan Kitchen*, reprinted with permission.

1 cup corn kernels, fresh or defrosted frozen
1 cup water
1 celery stalk, chopped
1 small onion, chopped
1 small bell pepper, chopped (optional)
1 carrot, ripple-sliced or sliced 3/16 inch thick
3 medium white potatoes, ripple-sliced or sliced 3/16 inch thick
1/4 cup fresh parsley, minced (packed)

Preheat the oven to 350 degrees F. Oil a 9-inch square baking pan. Place the corn and the water in a blender and process until smooth and milky.

Place the celery, onion, and pepper, if using, in a bowl and mix. Put half the celery mix in the pan. Spread half the sliced carrot in an even layer over the celery mixture, then layer half the potato slices over the carrot. Repeat with remaining ingredients to create another layer of celery mix, carrot, potatoes, and top with the minced parsley. The total depth of the vegetables in the pan should be about 1 3/4 inches (not more than 2 inches).

Pour the corn milk into a medium saucepan over medium high heat. Bring the corn milk almost to a boil, stirring and scraping the bottom to prevent scorching. Pour the corn milk evenly over the vegetables. Cover the pan with aluminum foil or a cookie sheet. Bake 1 hour or until the potatoes are tender and a knife slides in easily. Remove the cover. Broil 3 to 5 minutes to lightly brown the top.

Nonvegan Flips for Vegan

lifetime vegan woman + meateating intermittent vegetarian man =>
vegan woman + vegetarian man
Adair and Nick Moran

Adair Moran and Nick Little were cast together in a national tour of a children's theater production, *Ramona Quimby*. They gradually evolved from "eating together" or "watching a movie together" to "dating." They married in 2005.

Adair was raised vegan and has been vegan all her life. She maintains a vegan diet primarily because she loves animals and does not want to see them harmed. She also likes the health and environmental benefits. Being on the road together and working in a lot of small towns, Nick saw Adair working hard to maintain a vegan diet in less-than-ideal circumstances.

Nick was already not a big meat eater. He had been vegetarian about six years, but had gone back to eating meat for convenience when touring the country doing a very athletic one-person show. "I've always had a very high metabolism, and it just got to the point where I was tired of putting the time and effort into finding decent vegetarian options when traveling through areas where vegetarian options are limited," says Nick. "Eating meat tends to be habit-forming. Once I started eating meat again, I didn't stop until Adair brought the subject up some years later."

They were always cooking vegan food and going to vegan or vegan-friendly restaurants together. He gradually started eating less meat. As their relationship progressed and they began to talk about things like living together and getting married, Adair expressed a preference for a vegetarian household. "When things started getting serious, I let him know that I didn't think I could be married to a non-vegetarian." Since Nick had previous experience with a vegetarian diet, he was open to this.

Nick is now an ovo-lacto-vegetarian who loves cheese and admits to missing good kielbasa. He credits Adair's influence for cutting meat out of his diet. "If he went totally vegan I'd want it to be because he believed in it, not because I made him do it," says Adair, who notes that Nick has switched from milk to soymilk.

Nick has found ways to satisfy his occasional cravings for hearty, meat-like things. For example, he and Adair go to a vegetarian restaurant that makes a soy vegetarian fried chicken so good that Nick says it satisfies all of his fried chicken cravings. They live in New York City where they frequent favorite vegetarian restaurants. Their apartment is convenient to ethnic restaurants they like: Japanese, Ethiopian, Chinese, Thai, and Indian.

The couple has a very small kitchen, so dinner is usually simple, but definitely satisfying: loaded baked potatoes, big salads, veggie burgers or dogs with fries, pasta dishes with homemade marinara, vegetable curry, or hearty vegetarian soups and stews. "I'm a sucker for savory and/or spicy dishes. But it's not very often I have the time to make these things myself," says Nick.

When Nick does have time to cook, it is also appreciated. "He makes mean vegan pancakes," says Adair of Nick's Classic Pancakes .

As a nonvegan who dated and married a vegan, Nick expresses it as similar to other cultural or lifestyle differences. "Listen. Ask questions respectfully. Come with an open mind ready to learn. Learn to disagree without arguing. If you don't get the same in return, the person probably isn't worth your time."

Nick's Classic Pancakes

Yield: 15 (4-inch) pancakes

Classic pancakes are very simple. The art of making good pancakes is all about controlling the batter thickness and heat. Thick batter + lower heat = a thicker, more cake-like result. Thinner batter + higher heat = thinner, crispier, more crepe-like result.

2 cups whole wheat pastry flour or unbleached white flour
2 Tablespoons raw cane sugar crystals

2 1/2 teaspoons baking powder
1/2 teaspoon salt
3 Tablespoons plus 4 teaspoons vegetable oil
1 1/2 cups soymilk or nut milk plus extra as needed

Place the dry ingredients in a large bowl and mix. Add 2 table-spoons of the oil. Add the soymilk gradually while stirring to get the desired consistency without lumps (see note). Place 1 table-spoon oil in a large skillet over high heat. The pan is hot enough if a drop of water spatters when flicked onto the surface (stand back). Reduce the heat to medium or medium-low and pour 1/4 cup of bat-ter per pancake into the pan (2 or 3 pancakes per typical pan). Cook the pancakes for approximately 3 minutes or until bubbles come everywhere through the batter and the underside is golden brown. Flip the pancakes and cook them for another 2 to 3 minutes or until they are golden brown on both sides. Remove the pancakes and serve warm.

Repeat with the remaining batter, adding 2 teaspoons more oil between every two batches of pancakes, or more often if necessary. Move the oil around the pan so it is completely coated. The batter thickens as it stands; add additional soymilk as necessary to pro-duce the desired consistency.

Nick's notes: Basically substitute soymilk or nut milk for the milk in a nonvegan pancake recipe, and drop the egg. This is also a bit more baking powder than in a typical recipe which helps com-pensate for the lack of egg by making the pancakes lighter and air-ier. (The binder of the egg helps trap gas bubbles in the pancakes as it cooks). I've experimented with using thickeners like arrowroot and cornstarch to substitute for the egg, but nothing has worked as well as simply adding more baking powder.

… and I'm not a big fan of trying to gussy up such simple fare with innovative ingredients.

Do not mix the batter any more than is needed to completely combine the ingredients. Mixing too much activates the wheat gluten and creates chewy, doughy pancakes (ick). For this reason, never use an electric mixer for pancakes.

Author's Notes: Nick's Classic Pancakes are terrific as simple pancakes. For those of us who just can't resist the urge to be innovative, this recipe works well with chocolate chips or sliced bananas. Use blueberries in pancakes that are thick enough to contain whole blueberries. Top with vegan margarine and maple syrup, and add fruits such as banana, peaches, strawberries, and other berries.

Truly adventurous folk can try these pancakes as a savory item: Halve the sugar, double the salt, and add herbs such as 1 tablespoon Italian seasonings to the mix. Serve with mashed avocado and a hint of lemon juice for a delightful meal. Stir-fried mushrooms also top the pancakes well.

Nick and Adair

Smitten from the Start

vegetarian woman + meat-loving man =>
vegan woman who cooks meat for him + nonvegan man
Anne and Angus Watkins

Angus Watkins met Anne on a chance encounter in a bookstore in 1993. Immediately intrigued with each other, they discovered a shared love of family, adventure, environmentalism, travel, laughter, and social justice. Their first real date was at Forest Lawn Cemetery in Buffalo, across from the office where Anne worked. For a vegetarian picnic during her lunch hour she brought sandwich makings: bread, cheese, lettuce, tomato and onions, and some fruit.

On their first date she realized he was the one for her. "We had so much in common, our values and dreams," says Anne. "I was just overwhelmed that I had found such a wonderful person. At age forty-six I was totally smitten. I remember going back to work after our date with a glow for the rest of the day. He had lived an unusual life and had so many qualities that I admire, such as leadership, the ability to write (outstanding poet), a creative talent, and a wonderful ability to relate to people."

Anne mentioned during that date that she was vegetarian. At the time Angus accepted it as who she was. However, as they got closer and started spending more time together, it became an issue. "Angus is an omnivore, not just a meat eater but a meat lover!" As the couple began eating more meals together, especially after they got married, he resented the constraints put on him by being married to a vegetarian. His real pleasure in eating was meat, and he often asked if she would try a little piece of steak or fried fish. "I think he took it as a criticism of him personally that I was 'above' eating food he liked. I have generally cooked meat for Angus and accepted that he enjoyed it. It wasn't a problem for me that he ate meat, as much as it was a problem for him that I didn't eat meat."

When Anne became vegan, their food choices became even more of an issue for Angus who recalls, "She was on 'an extreme diet.' We couldn't even go out to eat at restaurants or go to friends' houses for dinner without a lot of limitations or advance planning!" Angus likes to cook and at first felt there was nothing he could prepare that would suit her vegan diet, but he made the effort. Angus is increasingly aware of the ethical and health implications of moving toward plant-based meals. He enthusiastically eats her tantalizing vegan food. And he appreciates the fact that she prepares meat for him. "I admit the ethical problems of eating meat, but enjoy the textures and flavors."

When Anne and Angus were first dating, a typical meal included macaroni and cheese, a few cooked vegetables, a potato or rice, bread and butter, and probably a piece of meat for him. Anne loves to bake, so there would have been a rich dessert. Now a typical meal includes a rice and bean dish such as the scrumptious Watkins' Yellow Rice with Black Beans; a vegetable or two, preferably in season; a salad; and occasionally a meat dish for him. Dessert is likely to be pie or a fruit dessert.

"We love, respect, and admire each other. We see one another as life companions," says Angus. "The differences we have surrounding food choices have been challenging at times, as have other diverging interests. We are united in our desire to accommodate, support, and help the other. I look forward to the ongoing adventure of growing, discovering, and fun in years ahead!" (Watkins' photo p. 109)

Watkins' Yellow Rice with Black Beans

Yield: 4 servings

Anne Watkins says, "It's so simple! I adapted the recipe from friends who invited us to their house for dinner."

Rice:
2 cups water
1/4 teaspoon salt
1/4 teaspoon onion powder

1/4 teaspoon garlic powder
1/4 teaspoon turmeric
1 cup basmati rice, brown or white

Beans:
1 can (15-ounces) black beans with liquid
2 Tablespoons olive oil
1 Tablespoon balsamic vinegar
1 Tablespoon dried oregano
1 Tablespoon dried basil

Topping:
1 fresh tomato, diced
1/4 cup chopped fresh parsley
1/4 cup chopped red onion or white Vidalia onion.

For the rice: Place the water in a medium saucepan. Add the salt, onion powder, garlic powder, and turmeric to the water and bring it to a boil over high heat. Stir in the rice, cover, reduce the heat to simmer until the liquid is absorbed, about 45 minutes for brown rice or 15 minutes for white rice. Remove the saucepan from the heat and let the rice stand, covered, for 5 to 10 minutes.

For the beans: While the rice is cooking, place the beans, oil, vinegar, oregano, and basil in a medium saucepan, stir, and cook for 20 minutes over low or medium-low heat, until much of the liquid has evaporated.

For the topping: Stir the tomato, parsley, and onion together in a small bowl.

To serve, spoon the rice onto a platter or large, shallow bowl, then spoon the black bean mixture over the rice (making sure some rice shows around the edges) and top with the tomato mixture.

Note: Instead of making your own rice, you can use one package of yellow rice mix. (Be sure to check the package, as some of them are made with chicken stock.) Cook according to the package directions.

Carrots and Wings

vegan man + carnivorous woman =>
vegan man + omnivorous woman yet eager vegan experimenter

Dude Hamre and Barb Johnson

"I was eating wings. He was eating carrots. It was all good," Barb Johnson recalls of meeting Dude Hamre at a sports bar near Erie, Pennsylvania. Barb says she was drawn to his kind, warmhearted, gentle, sweet, caring personality. Of Barb, Dude says, "She's cool. She's laid-back, easy-going, humorous, compassionate, and affectionate." Barb and her dog, Duncan, eat meat while Dude and his two rabbits, Kelly and Calvin, are vegan.

Dude informed Barb that he is vegan a few days after they met. She was going to fix him chicken and he suggested tofu instead. "I think he fixed me a curried tofu with rice dish," Barb says.

"You can bet it was something tasty," chimes in Dude.

Barb does most of the cooking. "I like cooking with TVP (textured vegetable-soy protein): tacos, goulash, chili, spaghetti. It has the same taste and texture as hamburger. It's easy to cook, quick, no grease, easy to digest, and the vegan will eat it."

Barb does most of their food shopping and pays more attention to ingredients since Dude became part of her life. "He just happened to come in at the right time. God takes care of me. I had an operation in October 2003 that required dietary changes and met Dude in December. I don't eat as much meat and processed foods as I used to. He was a godsend because he helped me out and made it much easier. If they came up with a TVP that tasted like chicken wings, I'd eat it. I still like eating meat, eggs over easy, and a specific brand of hot dogs. I learned about TVP from him so I don't feel like I've had to change much."

I am the only vegan Dude and Barb hang out with socially. He often fields questions about why he is vegan, to which he responds that it is for the creatures and for his health. He restrains himself from telling people that they are killing themselves. Often the conversation leads to questions like "What do you eat? Tofu?" He talks of the bounty of flavors the average American has not sampled, including his favorite Middle Eastern foods: tabouli, hummus, couscous, baba ganoush, falafel, pita bread, and zatar bread.

The secret to their happiness and compatibility in their vegan with a nonvegan relationship? According to Barb, "I don't think it has anything to do with food. It's just getting along and having the same interests. Food's pretty easy. He doesn't mind if I eat meat. And I don't mind if he eats meat either."

"I would prefer if you didn't eat meat, but it's not a deal breaker," Dude adds. "We both let each other be who we are. It's pretty cool."

In the summer Dude and Barb like to dine on a salad of red leaf lettuce, romaine lettuce, kale, celery, cucumber, broccoli, mushrooms, carrots, olives, tomatoes, fennel, fresh herbs: spearmint, pineapple mint, marjoram, thyme, arugula, parsley, basil, oregano, and cilantro. All the ingredients come from Dude's garden except the mushrooms and olives. A main attraction may be Barb's Orange TVP "Chicken" while a favorite dessert is vegan blueberry ice cream.

Barb's Orange TVP "Chicken"

Yield: 6 to 8 servings

This looks like a long recipe, but it is actually three easy recipes in one that together make a full meal.

To make the "Chicken"
2 1/2 cups vegetable stock or water
1 1/2 cups TVP (textured vegetable-soy protein) "chicken" chunks
1/4 cup soy sauce
1/4 teaspoon salt
1/4 teaspoon black pepper

1/2 cup cornstarch (optional)
1/3 cup olive oil (optional)
1 Tablespoon soy sauce (optional)

Place 2 cups of the stock and the TVP in a large nonstick saucepan and cook over medium-high heat, stirring frequently. When the TVP has absorbed all the stock add the remaining 1/2 cup stock gradually as needed. After the initial stock, the TVP should never be soupy.

Juice both oranges and include the pulp. Grate the outer surface of the orange peel (orange, not white) to acquire 1 tablespoon zest. Add the orange juice, zest, soy sauce, salt, and pepper to the TVP. The TVP should be tender to the taste.

Continue to cook 20 to 30 minutes stirring more frequently as the mixture becomes drier, until the TVP is brown and slightly caramelized, and smells delicious.

To fry the "chicken" (optional procedure):

Put the cornstarch in a mixing bowl. Toss the cooked TVP in the cornstarch. Put the oil in a large skillet over medium heat. When the oil is hot, toss the TVP into the oil. Stir frequently. Cook the TVP about 10 minutes, until slightly crispy, adding the soy sauce to the TVP when it is almost done.

Place some paper towels on a plate. Pour the "chicken" onto towels and blot off any excess oil.

Rice with Veggies

4 cups vegetable stock or water
2 cups long-grain white rice
Juice of 1 orange
1 carrot, chopped
1 small head broccoli, chopped

Place the stock and rice in a large saucepan and bring to a boil over high heat. Add the orange juice, carrot, and broccoli. Cover, reduce the heat to simmer 20 minutes or until the rice is tender and the stock has been almost completely absorbed.

Orange Sauce
    1/2 cup orange juice
    1 teaspoon cornstarch
    1 Tablespoon ketchup or tomato paste
    1/8 teaspoon ground ginger
    1 hot red chili pepper (optional)
    1 teaspoon spicy mustard (optional)

Place the orange juice and cornstarch in a small saucepan and mix until smooth. Add the ketchup and ginger. If using chili pepper and mustard, add them. Mix. Bring to a boil over high heat, stirring constantly to prevent sticking. Remove from the heat. Remove the pepper before serving.

Serve TVP "Chicken" over Rice with Veggies. Top with Orange Sauce and garnish with parsley. Use soy sauce as condiment.

Dude and Barb

Two of a Kind

red meatless man + nonveg man => wishy-washy vegetarian man + vegetarian man => 2 vegetarian men => 2 vegan men

Ed Coffin and George Sampson

Ed Coffin and George Sampson met through a mutual friend when Ed was seventeen and George was eighteen. George was a meat-eater while for health reasons Ed had not eaten beef or pork since age ten. On dates they went out to eat and loved sushi. They moved in together . One night Ed came home and George showed him a video online of animals being slaughtered. The video said to "go vegetarian" at the end, so that is what they did.

While they still consumed dairy and eggs, Ed became more interested in his food choices. He began looking up vegan websites and podcasts. Ed found "Vegetarian Food for Thought," a podcast by Colleen Patrick-Goudreau. One episode was about the cycle involved in milk production—cows are made pregnant and their babies are taken. Ed immediately informed George and they went vegan on the spot.

"When we both became vegan at the same time after being together for two and a half years, it became obvious to me that I couldn't settle for anything less than this level of ethical decency towards other sentient beings," says Ed. "I realized how lucky I was to be with someone who thinks rationally and puts his ethics into action. He wasn't doing it for me, but for the animals. That moment I realized he was the one for me."

"Eating food has never been more delicious and as much of an adventure as it has been since we became vegans," Ed continues. "To say our dates revolve around food is an understatement. Our dates now consist of us trying to eat at as many new vegan places as we can. The last time we did this, I think we ate at two different vegan ice cream places in the same day!"

"It is easy to be vegan today," George adds. "Many meat-eaters think that vegans miss out on the great foods they used to love; this is not true. We get delicious vegan buffalo wings at a local Philadelphia restaurant, the best vegan cheesecake is only a few blocks away, and everything else I love can be bought or made." George has inspired many friends and relatives, including his mother and sister, to go vegan.

Ed and George are both full-time students, full-time workers, and animal activists. Ed is studying to become a registered dietician while George is studying finance. Ed credits his background in nutrition and his love of cooking for the ability to prepare healthy homemade vegan meals. He tests new recipes on George, including his amazing Tiramisu.

Ed and George spread the vegan message and work towards their vision of total animal liberation. They feel that the oppression and exploitation of animals is very similar to the discrimination homosexuals face in our society. Ed, George, and their friends formed a new non-profit in Philadelphia named Peace Advocacy Network. P.A.N. works on animal rights issues and other social justice issues, like the environment, sexism, racism, heterosexism, and human hunger.

The main factors in a successful same-sex relationship are the same as in any other relationship. Ed and George's secret to a great long-term relationship is balance. Realizing that moods fluctuate means not taking little insults personally. It is important to be able to recognize what is not worth the argument. No matter who is going to take out the trash or clean the house, at the end of the day Ed and George enjoy sharing a delicious vegan dinner together.

"Becoming vegan is, perhaps, the best thing that has ever happen to us. It has opened our eyes and made us more compassionate," says George. "We have many vegan friends who share our values about injustice to animals and other social issues. Veganism is common ground that has brought Ed and me closer together and has given us purpose."

Tiramisu

Yield: 8 servings

This is an incredibly decadent dessert that really impresses people with its authentic taste.

1 9-inch Vanilla Cake, chilled
2 cups very strong coffee, cold (triple brew or use French press)
3 cups Creamy Coconut Whipped Topping, chilled
1 1/2 ounces dark chocolate

Cut the cake into 1-inch-thick strips. Pour the coffee into a bowl. One at a time, dip strips of cake into the coffee very briefly and place in the bottom of a 9-inch square glass pan. Use your hands to push the moist cake down and spread it out to cover the bottom of the pan. You should use about half of the cake.

Spread half of the whipped topping over the moist cake layer. Using a grater or a knife, shave the chocolate. Sprinkle half of the chocolate over the topping layer.

Repeat with the remaining cake, topping, and chocolate. Place the tiramisu in the refrigerator and chill for at least one hour before serving.

Vanilla Cake

Yield: one 9-inch round cake (8 servings)

You can glaze this cake, frost it, toss berries on it, or use it as a base for Tiramisu.

1 1/2 cups vanilla (or plain) soymilk
3/4 cup sugar
1/4 cup vegetable oil
2 Tablespoons lemon juice
1 Tablespoon ground flaxseeds
1 teaspoon vanilla extract
2 cups whole wheat pastry flour

1 1/2 Tablespoons baking powder
1/4 teaspoon salt

Preheat the oven to 350 degrees F. Oil one 9-inch round cake pan. Place the soymilk, sugar, oil, lemon juice, flaxseeds, and vanilla in a large bowl and whisk them together. Place the flour, baking powder, and salt in a separate container and mix. Combine the two mixtures and mix. Bake for 35 minutes or until a toothpick pushed into the center comes out clean. Cool cake before serving.

Creamy Coconut Whipped Topping

Yield: 3 cups

Although not a "health food," this recipe offers a less processed, less expensive, and more delicious alternative to store-bought soy whipped toppings. It keeps in the fridge and does not break down at room temperature.

2 cans (14 ounces each) full-fat unsweetened coconut milk
1/2 cup confectioners' sugar
1 teaspoon vanilla extract

Place the coconut milk cans in the fridge for at least one hour. Do NOT shake coconut milk. Remove the lids and spoon the solid portion of white coconut milk into a large bowl, leaving the transparent water behind in the cans. Add the sugar and vanilla. Whip the ingredients together. Using a handheld electric mixer on high speed for 2 minutes is easy, although whisking with a whisk or fork for a few minutes until smooth will also work.

Note: When purchasing coconut milk, the more expensive brands tend to work better because they have less water. Buy brands without emulsifier in the ingredients because separation of the solids from the liquid is essential.

Lifelong Companions

lifetime vegan woman + meat-relishing (former vegan) man =>
2 vegans

Heidi and Daniel Fox

Both Heidi Graff and Daniel Fox were raised vegan from birth. They met at a conference of the North American Vegetarian Society (NAVS). Daniel was a few months old. Heidi was five years old and recalls he was a cute baby. When Heidi was seven and Daniel was two, she remembers telling her mom, "When I grow up, I'm gonna marry him!" They share a common bond because their parents were actively involved in NAVS.

Heidi has always appreciated being vegan. "I like to protect animals and let them have long and happy lives. I don't do it so much for health reasons. It's totally an animal rights choice," she says. "I can't imagine eating animals because they are my friends. My parents always gave me a choice when I was at friends' houses about what I wanted to eat. My friends were receptive to my veganism and never pressured me. It might be easier for me being a female to be vegan. Often females are on diets. Caring about animals is cool for women. Men get more pressure to be strong and tough and eating meat is often part of that."

From age twelve to twenty-one Daniel was not vegan. "I tried a Big Mac and it tasted good. I was suppressing all feelings about anything, including compassion for animals. I didn't really think about it. I didn't make the connection between what I was eating and where it came from." Until that time being vegan was just standard in his life.

By the time they were twenty-one and twenty-six, Daniel and Heidi started hanging around together a lot. Heidi's love for animals began to have an increasing influence on Daniel. When he stopped to think about what he was eating, it bothered him. "I believe animals have souls and feelings, just like people. I wouldn't want someone to torture and kill and eat me so I don't want to do it to the animals."

The two were close friends for years, visiting on weekends with friends or on cookouts with parents. Daniel proposed romantically on World Vegetarian Day, October 1, 2003. "I made her close her eyes. I drove her to the woods near her parents' house. We walked fifty feet to a clearing, which was the site of our first kiss. When she opened her eyes I was already on one knee. I did not have the ring till a week and a half later, but the date was more important than anything." They married exactly two years later.

"I love Daniel's cooking. He likes to cook pasta. He would eat it every day if he could. I prefer it less often. Foxy Fudge is a favorite delicious treat. In the summer he makes me salads for work with yummy fresh vegetables," Heidi says. The couple's favorite dates include movie and dinner at a restaurant—Chinese, Japanese, Indian, or a pizza place. They especially enjoy games nights together with friends.

The secret to their relationship is not in the food. "Daniel and I are happier together than a lot of people are because we love spending time together. Our beliefs about important things are the same: veganism, how to treat animals, how to treat people. We genuinely love each other, trust each other, talk about everything."

Foxy Fudge

Yield: 16 servings

This fudge is ridiculously easy. It only tastes complicated.

2 cups chocolate chips
1 cup nut butter such as almond, cashew, or peanut

Melt the chocolate chips in a double boiler over medium high heat, stirring constantly. Add the nut butter and stir until melted and well mixed.

Lightly oil an 8-inch square baking pan. Pour the melted fudge into the pan. Place it in the refrigerator and let cool for several hours to set. Cut the fudge into 2-inch squares and serve.

Daniel and Heidi

The Odd Couple

vegan woman + hunter/fisherman =>
vegan woman + great vegan cook with his meat on the side
Jennie and Dan Kerwood

Jennie Kerwood is a vegan, animal rights activist, and past-president of the North American Vegetarian Society (NAVS). Her husband Dan is a sport fisherman/hunter who belongs to the NRA and an indoor shooting team. She orders her veggie pizzas without cheese; he loads his with sausage and mozzarella. He's a conservative Republican; she's a liberal Democrat. While he listens to rock 'n roll, she prefers folk music. He's Catholic; she's Jewish; they held a Methodist wedding.

So what prompted these two opposites to tie the knot? It is really pretty simple. They bring out the best in each other. Together they learned to stretch in directions they thought weren't possible.

Their potluck wedding reception featured both vegan and non-vegan offerings and a contra dance courtesy of some musician friends. With vegan food on one side of the room, nonvegan on the other side, Jennie solved the problem of keeping everyone happy without buying meat herself. She noticed how many nonvegan friends happily sampled vegan items.

Despite their deep affection for each other, living together has its share of challenges, which in turn requires some creative coping strategies. Dan has to brush his teeth after eating meat, for example, or Jennie won't kiss him. While she still shudders routinely at the sight of dead-animal parts in her previously vegan home, they have found a way to make it work. "Part of our 'prenuptial agreement' was that any meat or cheese he brings into the house has to live in one drawer of the refrigerator, where it can't touch anything of mine," Jennie explains.

The secret to a harmonious vegan/nonvegan relationship is tolerance," Jennie says. "Even when it is a challenge. Dan and I are so well suited in other aspects, but veganism really does matter to me.

I would prefer a life partner who sees the world like I do, but we are who we are. We have marvelous fun together, and we enjoy each other's company. It is a compromise, and I don't think I could do it for anyone else except him."

"When we dined out, he ate what he wanted. At my house it was vegan," Jennie says. "But when we got married, I thought it was important for us to have an 'our' house, where we both could be who we truly are, which means my home is not vegan any more."

Dan is the primary cook in their relationship and still cooks for both of them pretty much every day. "Dan thinks most vegan recipes are fine, in general, but he doesn't really enjoy meat substitutes. They don't interest him. So he sticks to things that are vegan in their own right, not meat 'wannabes.'" Most days there is something vegan in the slow cooker waiting for Jennie when she gets home from work.

Dan's No-Ham Split Pea Soup

Yield: 6 servings

The couple's favorite meal is delicious in any version and can be made using a traditional stove method, explained first. Jennie likes to whip up her variation when she gets home from work using a pressure cooker. When Dan cooks he leisurely starts his in the morning and lets it cook all day in a slow cooker. Both ways they enjoy one-pot meals, simple clean ups, and dining together.

1 cup dried green or yellow split peas, picked over and rinsed
6 cups water
1 large white potato, chopped
1 large carrot, chopped
2 stalks celery, chopped
1 onion, chopped
2 cloves garlic, minced
1 teaspoon dried thyme
1 teaspoon salt
1/4 teaspoon ground black pepper

2 drops liquid smoke
2 drops red hot pepper sauce
2 cups chopped fresh greens such as kale, collard greens, spinach, Swiss chard, or bok choy

Place the split peas and water in a large saucepan. Bring to a boil over high heat then add the potato, carrot, celery, onion, garlic, thyme, pepper and salt. Cover and reduce the heat to simmer about 60 minutes, until the split peas are soft and "dissolve" when stirred, and the vegetables are tender.

Add the liquid smoke and hot sauce. Add the fresh greens and cook a few minutes before serving, until the greens are wilted. (Collard greens or kale take longer than spinach, chard or bok choy.)

Dan's Slow Cooker Variation:

Use only 5 to 5 1/2 cups water, depending on desired thickness. Bring soup ingredients (except greens) to a boil at high heat, reduce to low heat and simmer at least 4 to 6 hours. Dan always includes all the seasonings, never the greens.

Jennie's Pressure Cooker Variation:

Use only a new style pressure cooker; not an old-fashioned "jiggle top" cooker. Use only 5 to 5 1/2 cups water, depending on desired thickness. Add peas, potatoes, carrots, celery, thyme, salt, and pepper. Cover and heat on medium high until the cooker gets up to full pressure, then reduce heat to low and simmer for 15 to 20 minutes. Remove from the heat.

Let the soup sit in the cooker until the pressure is released. Check that the split peas and potatoes are soft. If they are not soft, bring the soup back up to pressure and let it steam out again. Cooking time varies with pressure cookers.

Add the greens. Mix well. Simmer without the lid for 5 minutes to wilt greens. Jennie always uses the greens, not the onion, garlic, smoke, and hot sauce.

Vegan Evolution

vegetarian woman + nonveg man => 2 vegetarians => 2 vegans

Jo and Michael Stepaniak

Jo Stepaniak is a rare vegan gem, who inspires people with her sixteen dazzling books on vegan living and cooking. Jo became a vegetarian in the mid-sixties when there were few books or other resources available on the subject. Her motivation was simply a deep feeling in her heart that killing and eating other animals was inherently wrong. She became vegan about sixteen years later, along with her husband, Michael.

They met when she was a teacher at a sheltered workshop for adults with multiple physical and mental challenges. Michael interviewed there for a production manager position; their eyes met, and it was literally love at first sight for both of them. Luckily, he got the job!

Their first date was a long hike in a state forest in West Virginia about a week after they met. "If I recall correctly, I packed a picnic lunch of hummus, pickle, and alfalfa sprout sandwiches on homemade whole wheat buns and fresh fruit for dessert," Jo says. "I told him right up front that I was a vegetarian. I don't think he said much in response—even though I was the first vegetarian he had ever met. I think our attraction for each other was so strong that he would have gone out with me no matter what."

Michael never challenged Jo or questioned her choice. He just "went with the flow," so to speak. He never ate meat around her, so it was not an issue. On the other hand, she literally wooed him with food. She was really big into cooking and making everything from scratch, including bread, yogurt, and mayonnaise, as well as sprouting and container gardening. Fortunately, Michael has always been a good eater and loves vegetables, so it was easy to please him. Over the years, he has consistently enjoyed what she prepared and his role as the primary tester of all the recipes for her cookbooks.

"When we decided to get married, I told Michael that I would not allow any meat in 'my' kitchen. It was 'mine' because, although Michael was involved with everything around the house from car care to cleaning to laundry, he was not yet willing to prepare food. He told me that he could live with not having meat in the house, but he didn't want me strong-arming him into becoming vegetarian. He told me that if he was ever going to be vegetarian, it would have to be his own decision, on his own terms, for his own reasons, and in his own time. I am very grateful that by the time we did get married (which was three months later, a total of six months after we met), he had made the choice on his own, with no coercion from me."

"I waited until we were married two years and he was well settled into the vegetarian way to bring up the idea of going vegan. Michael was very receptive to it, especially because the ethical component of being vegetarian was always his primary incentive. He felt that as long as I could continue to make tasty dishes, he was perfectly happy to become vegan, both in diet and lifestyle."

Michael and Jo believe there are several components to a successful relationship, each weighted the same: respect (for yourself and each other), trust, shared values, listening well, willingness to compromise, appreciation, kindness, gratitude, letting go of having to always be right, and picking your battles carefully. They also firmly believe that there are three essential parts to every relationship that must be given equal consideration and care: the two individuals themselves, and the bond they form together.

Michael and Jo have been vegan for so many years now that it is no longer what they do; it is simply who they are. Says Jo, "When veganism infiltrates every part of your being, there is no way to separate it from any other part. To us, being vegan seems like the most natural thing in the world."

Jo's Cornucopia Oat Burgers

Yield: 8 burgers

These simple, wholesome, extraordinarily tasty burgers are among Jo's favorite recipes from her cookbook *Vegan Vittles: Second Helpings*, reprinted with permission.

4 teaspoons vegetable oil, plus extra for cooking the burgers
1 cup chopped onions
1 cup rolled oats
1 cup fresh breadcrumbs
1 cup chopped walnuts
1/4 cup flour (any kind)
1 teaspoon dried sage
1/2 teaspoon dried thyme
1/2 teaspoon salt
1 1/3 cups boiling water

Pour the oil into a large, heavy skillet and place over medium-high heat. When hot, add the onions and cook and stir for 15 to 20 minutes, or until tender and golden brown. Watch closely and adjust the heat as necessary so the onions do not burn.

Place the oats, breadcrumbs, walnuts, flour, sage, thyme, and salt in a medium bowl, and stir to combine. Pour in the boiling water and mix well. Stir in the browned onions. Let rest for 10 minutes, or until cool enough to handle comfortably. Form into 8 patties (lightly moistening your hands will help keep the mixture from sticking to them). Place the patties on a sheet of waxed paper as soon as they are made.

Add a layer of vegetable oil to a clean skillet (or the same skillet used to brown the onions) and place over medium heat. When hot, add the patties and brown them well on both sides, turning once.

Keys to Success

2 Standard American Dieters => vegan woman + nonvegan man

Kim Johnson and Rusty Gardner

The key to successful dating or marriage: "Respect is absolutely essential for any relationship to work. If you respect someone you show them that they are okay just the way they are. You love them as they are, not how they'd be after you fix them," Kim Johnson explains.

In 1991, a friend introduced her to Rusty Gardner. "I believe in the concept of chemistry. It's not necessary, but if it's there it's worth pursuing. I had an immediate attraction to Rusty," Kim remembers. On their first date they went ice skating and had dinner at a local bar. She ate a shrimp salad sandwich; he had crab cakes, traditional Maryland fare. When they were married in 1997, neither was interested in veganism.

After reading some stories on slaughterhouses, Kim began checking out more information on factory farming, primarily on the Internet. What really clinched it for her was reading about the battery hens and seeing pictures of those poor, wretched animals.

Rusty's sister Billie Gardner lives like the Gandhi quotation, "Be the change that you want to see in the world." Billie set an example of vegan life that inspired Kim to ask questions such as what she ate on a daily basis, how she got her protein and calcium, and her favorite meals. Kim became vegan although Rusty did not. "Life is too short to let minor differences create major problems. Don't let small things get in the way of having a relationship if the two of you are really drawn to each other," Kim says.

Kim and Rusty have changed through the years. "Love changes you, but you change because these are things you want to change in yourself. We should allow people to change in the way they want to. I can pursue veganism. He supports my choice," says Kim. Rusty has made significant changes in his personal eating habits to accommodate Kim's vegan decision. The couple eats a weekly average of three to four homemade meals together, two meals at a restaurant, and one carryout meal. Rusty enjoys eating vegan dinners, and he cooks vegan meals himself on occasion. One favorite is Kim's Really Fast After-Work Mediterranean Pasta .

Happily married couples continue dating. It is a way to remember to share quality time with each other beyond the dinner table at home. When Kim and Rusty eat out, sometimes he eats vegetarian, sometimes not. He doesn't want to become vegan because he likes dairy products such as milk, ice cream, and cheese. In their house they do keep milk, ice cream, honey, and cheese; the first two are Rusty's mainstays.

Rusty expressed his opinion on the key to successful dating and marriage: "Acceptance, tolerance, willingness, honesty, and openmindedness." Well said from a meat-eating man who married a meat-eating woman and now accepts, tolerates, and honestly supports Kim's choice to be a vegan. Rusty exhibits the willingness to understand her with an open mind. He eats vegetarian (putting cheese on otherwise vegan foods) at home, keeping companionship and sharing as the focus of meals.

Meanwhile, Kim appreciates Rusty's support for her compassionate choice. The battery hens and other creatures appreciate Kim's choice.

Kim's Really Fast After-Work Mediterranean Pasta

Yield: 4 servings

This recipe makes plentiful sauce for those who enjoy dipping bread while eating pasta. Kim serves it in a beautiful large pottery bowl.

1 pound thin pasta, such as angel hair
2 Tablespoons olive oil
1 clove garlic, minced, or 1 teaspoon dried minced garlic
2 cans (28 ounces each) diced plum tomatoes

1 can (15 ounces) artichoke hearts in water, drained and chopped
1/4 cup Greek olives, drained and chopped
2 Tablespoons capers, drained
1/8 teaspoon fresh ground pepper (optional)

Bring 4 quarts water to a boil in a large saucepan over high heat; add the pasta, and cook until just tender (or cook according to package directions). Drain.

Meanwhile, heat the oil in the saucepan over medium-high heat. Add the garlic. Cook 1 to 2 minutes until fragrant. Add the tomatoes, artichokes, olives, capers, and pepper, if using. Stir and cook 2 minutes or until the sauce is heated throughout. The sauce should be runny. Add the pasta to the sauce and toss to combine.

Rusty and Kim

Dating Vegans

Separate Spaces, Shared Values

vegan (lifetime vegetarian) man + kosher pesco-vegetarian woman
=> 2 vegans
Randall and Debbie Collura

Randall Collura was one of the vegetarian kids I grew up with at vegetarian summer conferences through the years. When I thought about vegan and nonvegan relationships, I thought it would be great fun to poke Randall's brain for a good story.

Randall was raised vegetarian but became vegan for the animals, "It's a simple choice; eating vegan does the least harm. Of course I was picked on for being different, but I developed a thick skin. I only dated one person in high school and she was vegetarian. There were other vegetarians at school."

Randall met Debbie at a Boston Vegetarian Society "dining out," a social gathering at a local restaurant, which was vegetarian friendly with a special vegan menu, for their first meal together. Debbie learned Randall was vegan when they met. "I try to be vegan," Debbie shares. "I grew up in a Kosher house. My original hesitancy about vegan was I didn't want to feel like I had another religion. Veganism is bigger than I am. I think it makes a lot of sense to be vegan. It's important to the planet. It's also because I love animals. The older I get the more important the animal issue becomes to me."

Debbie ate fish, but had not eaten meat since age eighteen. She was moving in the direction of vegan anyway. She didn't do dairy due to lactose intolerance. "I became more educated being around Randall and going to vegetarian events. I was being exposed to literature and health studies and the way animals are treated. It's easier to have the same diet being together. You eat, shop, and live together."

"We saw each other at the next dining out. We've been together ever since," Debbie explains. "We have both been married before so we were experienced in knowing what we wanted. We knew there was something there. It's not hard if you meet the right person. It was 'Ah, here you are!'"

Typical meals they fix for each other include Randall making pasta and Debbie making anything but pasta. Debbie discloses the details, "Randall typically makes pasta with vegetables and salad. Sometimes he makes dishes from his mother's cookbook, *Vegetarian Cooking for a Better World* (Muriel Collura-Golde). His best dish is Randall's Baked Eggplant, which he has been making since he was fourteen. I love eggplant. The first time he made it for me, I fell in love with it. He's been making it the same way ever since."

The real secret to their successful relationship is not the food. Randall explains, "Two bathrooms; we lived separately in our own spaces."

"Due to the distance between our jobs we had two separate households," Debbie continues. "We are combining households and moving into one house, but maintaining our separate spaces within the house."

Adds Randall (talking on the phone in **his** room), "Being vegan is about harmony, happiness, and compassion. Sharing these values with Debbie is the embodiment of our vegan lifestyle."

Randall's Baked Eggplant

Yield: 4 servings

So easy a monkey could make it!

1/4 cup olive oil
2 Tablespoons soy sauce
1 medium eggplant, sliced into 1/2-inch-thick rounds
1 1/2 cups tomato sauce

Preheat the oven to 375 degrees F. Lightly oil a 10 x 15-inch baking pan.

Put the oil and soy sauce in a small dish and whisk together. Place the eggplant rounds on the prepared pan and baste the tops with the oil mixture, using a pastry brush or small spoon.

Gently pour the tomato sauce onto each slice of eggplant and spread with a spoon. The sauce should cover each round almost to the edge. Bake for 30 minutes, or until the eggplant is tender. Serve with pasta, sourdough bread, and/or beans.

Debbie and Randall

The Kansas City Test

vegan woman + carnivorous man =>
vegan woman + vegetarian man
Victoria Moran and William Melton

William Melton ran a singles ad in the newspaper, just before the advent of Internet dating. Victoria Moran, reading the personals for amusement, was surprised to find herself drawn to one of them. In responding to the ad, Victoria was upfront that she had a daughter (Adair, p. 140), four cats and a dog, and that she was a vegan. She wanted to get the hard stuff out of the way first so if anything seemed problematic, it would all be out in the open.

Victoria and William met for the first time in a bagel shop. He was absolutely her type: Kris Kristofferson meets Eric Clapton. She had never dated a non-vegetarian before, but this seemed worth pursuing. William had never met a vegan but he accepted her way of eating without much thought. In those early days, it only seemed to him like a diet, not the philosophical underpinnings of a whole way of life. In the first two weeks of dating, William ate vegetarian whenever they went out—usually for Italian food, his favorite, and vegan-friendly for her.

When it was starting to get more serious, he took her to a sports bar for what she found out was a kind of test. When they arrived, a Kansas City Chiefs game was on TV and William had brought her a bright red Chiefs sweatshirt to wear. "I felt awkward and embarrassed," she recalls. "I'm just not a team-sweatshirt type. It was as if I was wearing a Halloween costume but it wasn't Halloween."

She ordered a salad and baked potato. William asked for a Kansas City steak. Victoria detached herself, thinking, "What the heck, it's not like we're getting married or anything." She survived the evening (with more anxiety about the sweatshirt than the steak). The next morning William called to say that he was done with meat.

"I'd never thought about what meat-eating really means until I met Victoria," says William. "All of a sudden it was clear to me that we shouldn't kill innocent animals for food we don't need. That sports bar date was just to be sure that I hadn't started falling in love with an extremist. Even though I was ready to be a vegetarian, my mother wasn't, and my children weren't. I didn't want to be with someone who couldn't give other people the freedom to make their own choices."

"I understand about not eating meat and fish, I've cut way back on dairy, and almost never eat an egg, but to commit to veganism is still a stretch for me," he says. "You've got to understand that I'm the kind of guy who, if I hadn't met Victoria, would be eating Big Macs. I've come a long way."

Although William's children, now young adults, eat conventionally, they were accepting of Victoria and her values from the outset. Once when they were driving together, Erik, then eleven, alerted everyone that a song by Moby had come on the radio. "He's a vegan like you," he told Victoria. That warmed her heart.

Victoria does believe, however, that being vegan made the "blended family" ideal much harder to achieve. It was a difficult transition and Victoria still wrestles with ways she might have done it better. "I became a vegan to live a more compassionate life, but I wondered so often when William's kids were young if maybe I would have shown more compassion by sitting down with them and eating a slice of pizza. In fact, I probably would have done that but I had my own vegan daughter to think about and the almost religious emphasis on reverence for life that I'd raised her with. The way I see it today is: If you're going to be a vegan, have a very stable life. The blended-family thing is tough for anybody, and throwing in something as unusual as veganism can make it a whole lot harder."

When retelling stories of successful couples, vegan with nonvegan, William and Victoria's shirt and steak story is one of the most helpful. William has been vegetarian for thirteen years now.

Victoria is a vibrant, healthy, fit, inspiring vegan who has authored ten books on wellness and personal growth, including *The Love-Powered Diet* and *Living a Charmed Life*. William wrote a screenplay, *Miss Liberty*, about a cow that escapes from a slaughterhouse.

Victoria's Famous Vegan Chili

Yield: 8 servings

If you like this chili as much as Victoria and William do, it is a meal in itself for four people. If you serve it with salad, chips and guacamole, and dessert, it can stretch to feed eight.

1 onion, chopped
4 Tablespoons olive oil
2 teaspoons minced garlic (optional)
1 red or yellow bell pepper, chopped
1 pound extra-firm tofu, drained, blotted dry,
  and chopped in 1/4-inch cubes
1 large can (32 ounces) or 2 small cans (16 ounces each)
  kidney beans
1 large can (approximately 30 ounces) or 2 small cans
  (15 ounces each) chopped or stewed tomatoes
1/2 teaspoon cumin
1/2 teaspoon chili powder
1/8 teaspoon cayenne pepper (optional)
1/8 teaspoon salt or salt-free seasoning (optional)
1 pound frozen corn kernels, preferably organic

Place the onion and 2 tablespoons of the olive oil in a large skillet over medium-high heat. Stir and fry 5 to 7 minutes, or until the onion becomes translucent. Reduce the heat to medium-low and add the minced garlic, if using. Cook 1 minute, stirring constantly. Add the bell pepper and continue cooking another 2 minutes, lowering the heat if necessary to keep the garlic from burning. Remove the vegetables with a slotted spoon and set aside.

Place the remaining 2 tablespoons oil in the empty skillet, add the tofu, and stir-fry over medium high heat about 5 to 7 minutes or until some sides are crisp. Add the beans, tomatoes, cumin, chili powder, to the tofu. If using cayenne and salt, add to the tofu. Stir. Add the veggies and frozen corn. Reduce the heat to simmer at least until warm throughout. The longer it cooks, the more the flavors meld together. An hour is fine as long as there is plenty of liquid (check occasionally).

Serve warm with cornbread or crackers. Also makes divine leftovers.

William and Victoria

Recipe Index

About the Author

Anne Dinshah is a lifetime vegan and author of *Healthy Hearty Helpings*, a vegan cookbook for busy people who wish to eat well. She coauthored Maribeth Abrams' cookbook *The 4 Ingredient Vegan*. Her career as a rowing coach takes her to a variety of locations throughout the United States where she embraces the challenges of everyday life with focus, persistence, and grace. Anne enjoys many forms of athletics from swimming to wrestling. She has been fortunate to become friends with many men and experience romantic dating adventures. With the help of nonvegan friends who appreciate her vegan cuisine, Anne is building her stone and timber-frame writer's cabin in western New York state. She is committed to building bridges as a vegan in a culture that depends heavily on animal products.